Answering Today's Problems

Yan Hadley

New Wine Press

PO Box 17
Chichester
West Sussex PO20 6YB
England

ISBN: 1 874367 33 7

Typeset by CRB (Drayton) Typesetting Services, Norwich.
Printed in England by Clays Ltd, St Ives plc.

Dedication

It is with much love that I dedicate this book to my wife Lorrainne and my two precious daughters, Claire and Naomi. Through the God-given gift of their lives to me, my experience and insight to living has been deepened more than I could possibly say.

Contents

Acknowledgements

I give thanks to all those who have played a part in helping me see published, this my second book. The support, hard work and encouragement of my wife Lorrainne, whose countless hours spent transposing my written notes on to the word processor has been deeply appreciated.

My gratitude goes also to Helen Cockram, together with Lexie and Bob Ellison, who willingly sacrificed their time to proof-read each chapter of the manuscript.

The invaluable assistance of my good friend of many years, Roy Knowles, has also been greatly appreciated. His consistent support, advice and expertise in the area of design for advance sales promotion, invoicing and labelling etc. has been a tremendous help.

Chapter 1

The Decline in
Values and Morality

On his last visit to Oxford, the great British Prime Minister W.E. Gladstone, sat in the senior common room of Christ Church College and talked at some length about the happy changes he'd witnessed in his lifetime. His outlook was so radiantly optimistic that it aroused a challenge from one of the students: 'Sir,' the young man said probingly, 'are we to understand that you have no anxieties for the future, are there no adverse signs that concern you?' The grand elderly statesman paused for a moment, then answered slowly, 'Yes, there is one thing which frightens me, it is that the fear of God seems to be dying out in the minds of man!'

That disturbing observation was certainly true then, but so much more today. As we look at the state of our nation, the fear of God is no longer in the hearts of people. The result of this is seen in the spiritual and moral decline within society. No longer can Britain be called, (if ever it could) a 'Christian Nation'. It would seem that all around us, at every level, we are witnessing the effects of a society that has turned its back on God. Nowhere is this more clearly observed than in what we are offered as a daily diet on our television screens. Programmes depicting murder, violence, fornication, adultery, infidelity, deceit, and rebellion against authority, only reflect what we have come to accept as a normal part of life.

We have drifted a long way from the standards once expressed in an inscription that still hangs in the entrance hall at Broadcasting House in Portland Square, London. It reads,

> 'To Almighty God: This shrine of arts, music and literature is dedicated by the first Governors in the year of our Lord 1931, John Reith being Director General. It is their prayer that good seed sown will produce a good harvest. That everything offensive to decency and hostile to peace will be expelled, and that the nation will incline its ear to those things which are lovely, pure and of good report and thus pursue the Path of wisdom and virtue.'

Regretfully these values have changed. We live in a hedonistic generation today – a generation that seeks pleasure, comfort and happiness regardless of the cost. There is always a price to pay though for sin, both individually and as a nation. The Bible says,

> *'Do not be deceived; God is not mocked, for whatever a man sows, that he will also reap.'*   (Galatians 6:7)

This is an eternal divine principle, one that is inescapable. It is a foolish thing to ignore that,

> *'Righteousness exalts a nation, but sin is a reproach to any people.'*   (Proverbs 14:34)

In our materialistic, godless society there is an urgent need to wake up to the fact that a nation is not made great by virtue of its wealth but by the wealth of its virtue!

According to data taken from the 1993 social trends report, issued by the Central Statistical office in London;

10

every day in Britain 470 babies are murdered by abortion. 480 couples are divorced. 90 children are taken into local authority care. 75 children will be added to the child protection register. 280 children run away from home or care. 27 school girls will become pregnant, (two under the age of 13) and every day 20 women are raped!

The report goes on to say that 65% of all videos for sale or hire deal with the occult, sex and violence. It states that one new crime is committed every six seconds, and a violent attack takes place every two minutes. There are two burglaries and three car crimes every 60 seconds! It is not surprising therefore that the report also says, each day, somebody calls the Samaritans every two minutes!

The Bible speaks of a similar decline in values and morality in Paul's letter to the Romans. As you read the first Chapter you could think that it was coming right from the pages of one of the Sunday newspapers! These verses highlight the shame of a godless nation.

All the problems in our world today can be traced right back to the statement which says,

> '*For the wrath of God is revealed from heaven against all ungodliness and wickedness of men who by their wickedness* **suppress the truth**.'   (Romans 1:18)

This is the beginning of the 'slippery slope'. Whenever we suppress, neglect or disregard the truth of God's word then turmoil and disorder become widespread, and the quality of life is affected. Where there are no moral absolutes, everything becomes relative and everyone does what is right in their own eyes. We notice in this chapter that as the truth is suppressed, an evil darkness gradually comes in and a downward spiral begins.

Firstly; verses 21 and 22 say,

> '... *for although they knew God they did not honour him as God or give thanks to him, but they became*

futile in their thinking and their senseless minds were darkened. Claiming to be wise, they became fools.'

When we suppress the truth of scripture we no longer acknowledge and honour God. Instead we become proud in our thoughts and begin to reject what God says in favour of our own ideas and concepts which are contrary to His word. The reality is that once people run away from the truth they fall victim to a lie! Humanism and rationalism begin to reign supreme and so we have a philosophy of man being the answer to his own problems.

Secondly; the next step down is idolatry in verse 23.

> *'. . . they became fools, and exchanged the glory of the immortal God for images resembling mortal man or birds or animals or reptiles.'*

God's place in a person's life is taken by something or someone else: it may be a physical statue or an imaginary deity. More commonly though, for the majority their god becomes money, power, possessions, ambitions or 'celebrities'. The end result is the same, God is replaced by something that man creates.

Thirdly; downwards we slide in verse 24,

> *'Therefore God gave them up in the lusts of their hearts to impurity, to the dishonouring of their bodies among themselves.'*

As the Lord lifts His protective hand off our lives, because of idolatry, our passions then become unrestrained. Immorality, lust and the abuse of the body with alcohol, drugs and sex become a plague on life. Permissiveness rules and so fornication and adultery become commonplace, resulting in the misery and heartache of broken marriages, one parent families and abortion on demand.

Fourthly; further still in verses 26 and 27 we find that society sinks deeper into a morass of vice.

> *'God gave them up to dishonourable passions. Their women exchanged natural relations for unnatural, and the men likewise gave up natural relations with women and were consumed with passion for one another, men committing shameless acts with men . . . '*

Sexuality now becomes confused and male and female distinction goes. Homosexual and lesbian relationships become normal and acceptable. Today we even have a 'Gay Movement' led by gay clergymen! There are thought to be over 400 avowed homosexuals belonging to the gay Christian movement who unashamedly proclaim homosexuality in the clergy ranks of the Church of England.

The degree of such promiscuity amongst heterosexuals as well as homosexuals result in a self-inflicted curse.

> *'. . . receiving in their own persons the due penalty of their error.'*   (verse 27b)

It is far from stretching the imagination to say that this speaks of the sexually transmitted diseases that are numerous and widespread today, not least of course, AIDS.

Fifthly; in verses 28–32 we read of the extent of man's inhumanity to man. Now at rock bottom we find depravity of all kinds.

> *'And since they did not see fit to acknowledge God, God gave them up to a base mind and to improper conduct. They were filled with all manner of wickedness, evil, covetousness, malice. Full of envy, murder, strife, deceit, malignity, they are gossips, slanderers, haters of God, insolent, haughty, boastful, inventors of evil, disobedient to parents, foolish, faithless, heartless, ruthless. Though they know God's decree that those who do such things deserve to die, they not only do them but approve those who practise them.'*

Today we are witnessing an appalling increase in cases

13

of child abuse, incest, rape attacks on the elderly, racial hatred and violence never before thought possible. There is fast coming a total breakdown in human relationships and we are becoming a 'Shock Proof' nation. Even as I write, our local evening newspaper carries the report of a sex attack on a pensioner, by a 12 year old boy! Also the chilling murder trial of two year old James Bulger has recently given its guilty verdict against two 10 year old boys. These were convicted of kidnapping and battering to death their tiny victim with an iron bar, then placing him on a railway line for his body to be mutilated. This latest incident stunned not just our nation but the world, leaving people asking the question, 'Where has society gone wrong?'

It was Sir Winston Churchill, another of our great Prime Ministers, who once said,

> 'You can trace the moral decline in our nation right back to the time when heaven and hell ceased to be preached throughout the land.'

People today seem to be so taken up with the immediate passing pleasures of the material, that they have lost sight of eternal issues. The awesome truth is that we are all accountable to God. The fear of the Lord is both the root and remedy of our problems. The absence of that fear lies at the heart of all decline in morality and values. But the road to recovery, and indeed to every problem that we face today, is found in the 'Positive Fear of God'.

What is the Fear of God?

To enable us to answer this important question, first we need to state what it is not.

(a)   The fear of God is not an optional extra to our lives, something that we can take or leave if we so wish. It is a definite command for us all. The Bible says,

14

> *'You shall fear the Lord your God; you shall serve him,*
> *and swear by his name.'* (Deuteronomy 6:13)

(b) It is not a negative feeling of being afraid to approach God. We are encouraged by the scriptures to approach the Lord with confidence and boldness. In Hebrews 10:22 it says,

> *'Let us draw near with a true heart in full assurance of*
> *faith, with our hearts sprinkled clean from an evil con-*
> *science . . .'*

(c) Also, the fear of God is not living with a slavish fear of punishment if we don't do what we should, serving out of a cringing sense of duty. The Bible says that each one of us should,

> *'Serve the Lord with gladness!'* (Psalm 100:2)

The fear of God is the most positive force a person can have in their life. It affects all that we do and say and influences what we think, where we go, the things we listen to and what we watch. It is a heart response of respect for the greatness, majesty and holiness of God, an expression of our love that shows an attitude of reverence for who God is. The fear of the Lord motivates people to righteous living and obedience so that they hate the things He hates and love the things that He loves. This is why we read,

> *'The fear of the Lord is hatred of all evil . . .'*
> (Proverbs 8:13)

Whilst it is true that the grace and forgiveness of God brings us into a right relationship with Him, it is the fear of the Lord that keeps us there!

Examples of Those Who Knew the Fear of God

The Bible is full of people who had a positive fear of the Lord in their lives. For the purpose of example though, we'll look at just four such cases, two from the Old Testament and two from the New.

Abraham

The promise from God to Abraham that he would at last, after many years of waiting, have a son, eventually came to pass. This was one of the most thrilling moments of his life. As this precious child grew up his relationship with his father must have been very close and special. Then one day God spoke to Abraham to test his obedience and called him to offer his son in sacrifice upon an altar. Abraham's reverence for God's word was such that he was prepared to go right through with this. Then at the very point where he had laid his son upon the altar, and was about to plunge the dagger into his heart, God stopped him saying,

> *'Do not lay your hand on the lad or do anything to him; for now I know that you fear God, seeing that you have not withheld your son, your only son, from me.'*
>
> (Genesis 22:12)

Job

Throughout generations this man has been a source of comfort and hope to countless people. The example of his life enduring the most awful trials brings also a challenge to us all. 'The patience of Job' is an expression known even to the unchurched. In the first chapter of the book of Job we find the secret of his strength.

> *'There was a man in the land of Uz, whose name was Job; and that man was blameless and upright, one who feared God and turned away from evil.'*   (Job 1:1)

The remarkable thing is that these words of praise were

16

not man's estimation of his life and character, but God's view of someone who walked with reverence and respect before Him.

The Early Church

In the book of Acts we find that the fear of the Lord was very much part of their lives. Far from being merely an Old Testament idea, it was central to the effectiveness and blessing of the New Testament Church. In Acts 9:31 it says,

> 'The Church throughout all Judea and Galilee and Sama'ria had peace and was built up; and walking in the fear of the Lord and in the comfort of the Holy Spirit it was multiplied.'

Jesus Christ

Here is probably the most striking example of someone who lived with the fear of God in their heart. Throughout His life this attitude reflected His relationship with God. We read,

> 'In the days of his flesh, Jesus offered up prayers and supplications, with loud cries and tears, to him who was able to save him from death, and he was heard for his godly fear.'   (Hebrews 5:7)

From these four examples we can begin to see whether or not we have the fear of God. These characteristics show us the degree of reverence and respect that needs to be developed in our relationship with the Lord.

As with Abraham, God looks for a willingness to surrender all, even the most precious thing that we have. Whether it be a relationship, a possession, our ministry or our own plans and desires. When the fear of the Lord is increasing in our lives there will be a complete obedience that doesn't hold anything back.

From the life of Job we find the evidence of our respect

for God is that we are blameless and upright in all that we do. Our lives express purity, holiness and a commitment to deliberately turn away from evil. Also even when we go through the most difficult of circumstances the positive fear of the Lord will be seen in an attitude to worship in spite of adversity.

When we look at the example of the Early Church we see the challenge of an uncompromising boldness to witness for Christ. Even in the face of persecution there must be nothing holding us back from having an effective, fruitful testimony. A life of inner peace and security, knowing the blessing of God is the reward for those who walk in the fear of the Lord.

As we consider Jesus, our perfect role model, we find someone who always had a clear knowledge of God's will. He lived with a definite sense of direction and purpose which came from His close relationship with God. This enabled Him to have the assurance not merely of offering prayers, but knowing those prayers would be answered.

The Benefits of Having the Fear of the Lord

Often when we examine our own lives in the light of scripture it is like looking into a mirror and seeing every spot and blemish. There appears to be a great gap between what we are and how we should be. Because of this there can come a feeling of self-condemnation. However, one of the most helpful ways to motivate us to live with a greater measure of the fear of God is to look at the exciting benefits that there are:

1. Knowledge
True knowledge doesn't come out of a text book or from a university education. Our own reasoning and logical thinking are important but not attributes that we can always trust. The Bible tells us where real knowledge is found.

18

'The fear of the Lord is the beginning of knowledge . . .'
(Proverbs 1:7)

I believe that a young boy on his knees in prayer, who has the fear of God in his heart, can see further than a godless professor standing on tip toe!

2. Wisdom

'The fear of the Lord is the beginning of wisdom . . .'
(Proverbs 9:10)

This basic understanding of how we acquire and grow in true wisdom is so far away from people's thinking today. There is a certain arrogance in the attitude of twentieth century man that scoffs at the need for God, or indeed anyone else to show them the way forward. This is expressed in the amusing observation of Mark Twain. He said,

'When I was 14 my father was so ignorant, I hated to have the old man around. But when I became 21, I was astonished to see how much my father had learned in only 7 years.'

3. Health

When someone is sick it doesn't automatically mean that they haven't got the fear of God. However, I do believe more people would be living in the benefit of divine health if the fear of God was in their lives. The Bible says,

'Be not wise in your own eyes; fear the Lord, and turn away from evil. It will be healing to your flesh and refreshment to your bones.' (Proverbs 3:7–8)

4. Prolonged Life

Again we see how our health is affected in that we are promised a longer life.

> *'The fear of the Lord prolongs life, but the years of the wicked will be short.'* (Proverbs 10:27)

We can of course all think of exceptions to this. Maybe godly people who have died at an early age, or perhaps an unrighteous person who has lived many years. However, as a general rule we have here a promise from the Lord that we can claim.

5. Confidence

This is a feeling and outlook that people long to have in a greater measure in their lives. We'll be considering the area of developing confidence in a later chapter because there are so many who struggle with this. It is a common battle that people have and yet the key is found right here in the Fear of the Lord. The Bible's promise is that we will know confidence by the degree of our respect for God. It says,

> *'In the fear of the Lord one has strong confidence . . .'* (Proverbs 14:26)

6. Happiness

In a world that appears at times very depressing, where people are dissatisfied and discontented, we can find in God complete fulfilment. The Bible says,

> *'Blessed, happy, fortunate . . . is the man who reverently and worshipfully fears the Lord always at all times (regardless of circumstances) . . .'* (Proverbs 28:14, Amp)

The word 'always' is very important, suggesting an attitude evident not merely on Sundays or in the Church, but a way of life in our daily experience.

7. Closeness with God and Revelation

Knowing God as a friend and not merely as someone who

is out there somewhere, remote and uninvolved in our lives, is one of the most thrilling things that a person can discover. The Lord revealing Himself personally to us is the promise of God's word and it comes as a benefit of knowing the fear of the Lord.

> *'The friendship of the Lord is for those who fear him, and he makes known to them his covenant.'*
>
> (Psalm 25:14)

8. Protection

We are living in perilous days and the Bible's clear counsel is that this world is going to get worse rather than better. As we live and serve the Lord we need the assurance of His protection and it is something that is given to us when we maintain a righteous relationship with God. His word says,

> *'The angel of the Lord encamps around those who fear him, and delivers them.'*
> (Psalm 34:7)

9. Provision

The final benefit for us to look at (though there are many others), is God's provision for all our needs. His instruction is,

> *'O fear the Lord, you his saints, for those who fear him have no want!'*
> (Psalm 34:9)

When Lorrainne and I got married, one of the hymns we chose for our wedding was, 'Great is Thy Faithfulness'. Over the years we've certainly proved the truth of those words together. Part of the hymn says, 'All I have needed thy hand has provided'. This is God's guarantee to all who live righteously and put their trust in Him. The Psalmist could write about this assurance from personal experience. David said,

'He provides food for those who fear him; he is ever mindful of his covenant.' (Psalm 111:5)

Where the Fear of God Needs to be Seen

(a) In Our Teaching

Through our words and by our example we have a responsibility to teach others respect for God. The need for this is great in our schools, homes and even in our churches. We read in Deuteronomy 31:12–13

> *'Assemble the people, men, women and little ones, and the sojourner within your towns, that they may hear and learn to fear the Lord your God...'*

In a day and age where rebellion and disrespect for all authority is common place, the fear of God needs to be taught to children from infancy. This is the only answer to a society in moral decline.

(b) At the Heart of Our Worship

Psalm 5:7 says,

> *'I through the abundance of thy steadfast love will enter thy house, I will worship toward thy holy temple in the fear of thee.'*

Worship within the context of the church is not just a 'happy clappy' time of noise, dancing and excited emotions. Praise God for all of those things: they are aspects of our worship that we need more of. However, they become empty and meaningless unless there is that attitude of reverence in all that we do.

(c) In Our Relationships

Our attitude to others in how we relate and react, is a good reflection of our relationship with the Lord. In 1 John 4:20 we read,

> *'If anyone says, "I love God," and hates his brother, he is a liar; for he who does not love his brother whom he has seen, cannot love God whom he has not seen.'*

So often there is division and discord between people. These wrong attitudes and contention often comes out of pride. This is why the words of Paul to the Church at Ephesus show us the importance of the fear of God in this area.

> *'Be subject to one another out of reverence for Christ.'*
> (Ephesians 5:21)

(d) Throughout Our Daily Work
In Colossians 3:22 it says,

> *'Obey in everything those who are your earthly masters, not with eyeservice, as men-pleasers, but in singleness of heart, fearing the Lord.'*

Frequently in the work place attitudes of disrespect and disloyalty towards employers are expressed. Grumbling and complaining is heard all too often. Today, glad willing service, coming from a spirit of excellence of wanting to do our best, even when no one is watching, is a rare thing. If we are to honour God though, in all we do, it is these righteous characteristics that express the reality of our respect for God.

(e) At Times of Temptation
All around us there are things that would seek to compromise our commitment to holiness, whether it be on the television, radio, in newspapers or simply the daily circumstances that we find ourselves confronted by. The fear of the Lord in our life is seen in the steps we take to keep

away from situations that would lead us into sin. The Bible says,

> *'By the fear of the Lord a man avoids evil.'*
>
> (Proverbs 16:6)

How to Develop the Fear of God

This must be seen as our personal responsibility. No one can do it for us. We must develop the fear of the Lord, that's why the Bible says,

> *'Since we have these promises, beloved, let us cleanse ourselves from every defilement of body and spirit, and make holiness perfect in the fear of God.'*
>
> (2 Corinthians 7:1)

Firstly; we must acknowledge the need to see ourselves as we truly are. Honesty about our life and reality before God is always the starting point for change. For king David, it was Nathan's confrontation with him over his sin with Bathsheba, that brought him to the place of reality (2 Samuel 12:1–7). David had committed adultery. Then in an attempt to hide what he had done he had Uriah, Bathsheba's husband, killed in battle, adding murder to his sin. When David realised his hypocrisy was exposed he confessed openly without excuse.

Secondly; a deliberate choice is needed. As an act of our will, we must commit ourselves to change. It is one thing to be convicted and to acknowledge our sin before God, but it is another thing to commit ourselves to doing something about it. God expects us to choose to live walking in the fear of the Lord. In Proverbs 1:28–29 we read,

> *'They will call upon me, but I will not answer; they will seek me diligently but will not find me. Because they hated knowledge and did not **choose** the fear of the Lord.'*

Thirdly; prayer must be our next step because in our own strength we cannot change ourselves. We need the help of God. It is as we call out to Him in prayer and ask, truly desiring to know His help, that His grace and strength comes. Just like the Psalmist, our hearts desire in prayer must be,

> 'Teach me thy way, O Lord, that I may walk in thy truth; unite my heart to fear thy name.' (Psalm 86:11)

God makes clear His willingness to instruct us as He says,

> 'Come, O sons, listen to me, I will teach you the fear of the Lord.' (Psalm 34:11)

Fourthly; taking some practical action and making an effort to do all we can personally to learn, expresses the genuineness of our desire. What is required is that we seek diligently and whole-heartedly to discover the fear of the Lord. Searching the scriptures, getting out a concordance, digging out those verses on the fear of God and dwelling on His character will require hard work but the reward will be great. Solomon when talking about this gives us the picture of a treasure hunt and says,

> 'If you seek it like silver and search for it as for hidden treasures; then you will understand the fear of the Lord and find the knowledge of God.' (Proverbs 2:4–5)

And so, even though all around gross darkness confronts us and the challenge of evil that faces humanity grows greater than in the days of Noah, there is hope. God's word through the prophet Isaiah speaks right into our situation today when he says,

> 'Arise, shine; for your light has come, and the glory of the Lord has risen upon you. For behold, darkness shall cover the earth, and thick darkness the peoples; but the

*Lord will arise upon you, and his glory will be seen
upon you. And nations shall come to your light, and
kings to the brightness of your rising.'* (Isaiah 60:1–3)

It is as we practice the fear of God in our lives that the
brightness of our testimony can begin to shine more
clearly and penetrate the darkness. We can make a difference!

Chapter 2

Religions' Broad Road of Compromise

The amusing story is told of a man, making his way home from the pub one night, somewhat 'worse the wear' for drink. Staggering through the darkness and singing at the top of his voice, he stumbled without noticing, into a cemetery. Precariously making his way down a narrow shadowy path he tripped over a shovel and fell into an open grave! Suddenly realising where he was, panic gripped him and he tried to claw his way out, but because of his drunken state and clumsiness it was hopeless. So he resigned himself to sitting back in the corner of this cold, eerie grave for the night.

Now, they say that troubles come in pairs, and it wasn't long before another drunk started to make his way home from an evening's drinking. Merrily singing, he made his way unknowingly into that same dark cemetery, staggered down that same narrow, shadowy path, tripped over the same shovel and fell into that same open grave! Terrified by where he found himself, he tried in vain to scramble out, when all of a sudden, from behind him in the shadows came a loud voice saying, **'You'll never get out!'** – But he did!

All too often people feel trapped by the darkness of their circumstances and are panicked into some course of action by the voices of their fears, anxiousness and despair. While it may seem to them that they have got out of one predicament it still doesn't change their real problem. As with the man in our story, he managed to get out of the grave but was still bound and captive to alcohol. The Christian gospel though, declares there is a way out of every problem people feel imprisoned by, and that people themselves can be changed also.

We, the Church, have a responsibility to make clear that the cause of today's problems is not political, social, environmental or financial, but spiritual. Only in an acknowledgement of our deep spiritual need for forgiveness of sin and a personal commitment to the claims of Jesus Christ can the answer be found. It was Jesus who said,

> *'You will know the **truth**, and the **truth** will make you free.'*
> (John 8:32)

In 'knowing' the truth of God's word people can experience His power to bring release. By accepting what the Bible says regarding ourselves and our need of Christ, people discover the miracle which changes not just their circumstances but their lives. When there is an openness to receive what the scriptures teach, then a breakthrough can come. This is why we read,

> *'The entrance of your words gives light . . . '*
> (Psalm 119:130, NIV)

Herein lies one of the major problems that hold people in bondage today. The Bible's authority is undermined and its truth distorted leaving people bewildered, not knowing quite what to believe.

The Fog of Confusion

It has been rightly said, 'If there is mist in the pulpit there will be fog in the pews!' 'Religion' presents such a broad road before those struggling to find a way out, that they are left confused about what is the truth, and therefore fail to discover the power that can bring freedom. Today we have numerous cults, sects and diverse philosophies in society. Also in our schools, comparative religions are taught with equal value being given to each. Life is like a confusing puzzle that has a missing piece. Until that one part is in its right place then we do not have a complete picture. This is what happens when Jesus Christ is not given His rightful position as Lord over all, especially in a person's individual life.

Unfortunately at times the nominal 'Church' only adds to the fog of confusion because some of its 'leaders' hold and express liberal views that are contrary to the word of God. We have 'unbelieving bishops' and so called 'Christian leaders', who amongst other things, deny the virgin birth, the miracles of the Bible, the bodily resurrection of Christ, the reality of heaven and hell and ultimately of course, the infallibility of scripture.

Not only does our multi-cultural, multi-faith society say there are many ways to God, but some churches would maintain this too. We are told to accept one another's beliefs, to be more tolerant, not so narrow minded and bigoted. It was the former Archbishop of Canterbury, Lord Runcie, who while in office besought us to, 'Look for the Holy Spirit in all religions and so work together for world peace!' This sounds very sensitive and accommodating but the fact remains, there is no such elasticity in the truth! All that we believe must be judged by what the Bible says and in how it relates to the exclusive sovereignty of Jesus Christ.

Once Christianity has no absolute truth to present and it begins to compromise, rather than give a definite moral and spiritual lead to the nation, it only adds to the darkness. We then have the situation that is spoken of in the Bible which Jesus condemned so strongly,

29

> '... if a blind man leads a blind man, both will fall into a pit.' (Matthew 15:14)

Multi-Faith Worship

At Winchester Cathedral in October 1987 a Creation Harvest Liturgy was held. This was an ecumenical Christian service to which members of other religions were welcomed as 'brothers and sisters in faith'. Everyone was invited to use 'as sources of prayer, inspiration and reflection,' readings from Bahai'sm, Buddhism, Hinduism, Islam, Sikhism, and Taoism. Over a thousand churches across Britain and the world used the service simultaneously that day, and a thousand in Britain since then.

In October 1988 there was a Creation Festival Liturgy at Coventry Cathedral. It displayed the influence of Hindu thought and again invited participants to use readings from various faiths for prayer. During the same month at Bristol Cathedral in an Inter-faith service the Bahai's affirmed that all religions were one. The Buddhists expressed their belief in security for the after life by good deeds and the Muslims listed Jesus alongside other prophets and said, 'We make no difference between one and another of them.'

In September 1989 at Canterbury Cathedral, a 'Festival of Faith and the Environment' service took place. Followers of different religions were invited to worship together. The organisers described it as a 'multi-faith event including a celebration which would draw on the teachings and beliefs of many faiths.' However, at the welcome service given to the pilgrims in the Cathedral, the name of Jesus was totally excluded.

Over recent years, in the various Commonwealth Day Observance services held at Westminster Abbey, multi-faith worship has been prominent. It has included worship of Brahma, Allah and Buddha but no worship of Jesus by name. Leaders also from Sikhism and other faiths have been encouraged to chant their prayers in their own languages. Jesus has not been mentioned in the hymns, the affirmations, the readings, the introduction, the meditation or even the blessing. On one of these occasions in March 1990 recognition was given to Him in just a couple of phrases '. . . through Jesus Christ our Lord,' at the end of two prayers by the Free Church and the Church of Scotland ministers. At the March 1991 service Jesus got only one mention. This was when the Rev. Dr Bill Davies, moderator of the Free Church Federal Council, inserted Jesus' name into a reading from the Beatitudes, although it is not actually in the original passage. Had he not done so, there would have been no use of the name of Jesus at all.

If people are going to find lasting answers to their problems it is crucial they come to understand that the road is not as broad as they have been led to believe. Jesus Christ spoke of only two ways in life. He said,

> *'Enter by the narrow gate; for the gate is wide and the way is easy, that leads to destruction, and those who enter by it are many. For the gate is narrow and the way is hard that leads to life, and those who find it are few.'*
> (Matthew 7:13–14)

With this blatant statement Jesus made clear that all people everywhere are travelling on one road or the other. The reality is that right now we are either totally going to hell or totally going to heaven. There is no grey area with the gospel and there can be no neutrality concerning Jesus Christ. The whole of the human race is divided, not by colour, class, culture, age or gender, but by who they acknowledge Jesus to be. The Bible teaches that He cannot be marginalized because He is the **only** Saviour for the world!

The Uniqueness of Jesus Christ

In our muddled, multi-faith society today, the urgent need

31

of the hour, if we are going to present a way out of the fog, is to lift up the matchless Name of Jesus. As we get back to God's word, which is, *'a lamp to our feet and light to our path'*, we can begin to find our way through the darkness. We have a unique message – one that is distinctive from all the religions of the world and Jesus Christ is at its centre. This is why the Bible says,

> *'He is the head of the body, the church; he is the beginning, the first-born from the dead, that in everything he might be pre-eminent.'* (Colossians 1:18)

Bamber Gascoigne, the well known television presenter and quiz master, though not a born again Christian, made an interesting comment in one of his books concerning his impression of Jesus. He said,

> 'Whether Jesus Christ be God, man or myth is uncertain, but one thing is sure, no other person has made such an impact on the history of the world as the man Christ Jesus.'

There can be no question about the historical fact of Christ's existence. Our very calendar bears testimony to this. It is 1994, that is one thousand nine hundred and ninety four years after the birth of Christ. His presence on earth split history, between BC and AD. Many historical documents have been discovered, (quite apart from scripture), that prove He existed. Also we can go into any library and read the works of Josephus. He wasn't a Christian, but a secular, Jewish historian who bears written testimony to Jesus Christ and the miracles He worked.

Even other world religions acknowledge the place of Jesus in history. Judaism accepts Jesus as a great Rabbi. Islam recognizes Him as a great prophet, second only to Mohammed. Buddhism respects Him as a great teacher and Hinduism sees Jesus as a manifestation of deity – one among many. The scriptures though, speak of Jesus as,

'... the bright morning star.'   (Revelation 22:16)

The morning star is that one light that is still shining when all the other stars have gone out. This is a marvellous picture of the uniqueness of Christ. When every other name and personality has disappeared from sight, Jesus will still be there! He stands alone, quite unlike any other. That's why the Bible says,

> *'God has highly exalted him and bestowed on him the name which is above every name, that at the name of Jesus every knee should bow, in heaven and on earth and under the earth, and every tongue confess that Jesus Christ is Lord...'*   (Philippians 2:9–11)

Firstly – *His Unique Birth*

Right from the beginning this was a supernatural and miraculous event: something that had never happened before and has never happened since. It was the fulfilment of what had been prophesied over 700 years previously. The prophet Isaiah spoke of it in saying,

> *'For to us a child is born, to us a son is given; and the government will be upon his shoulder, and his name will be called "Wonderful Counsellor, Mighty God, Everlasting Father, Prince of Peace."'*   (Isaiah 9:6)

The unique fact of Jesus being born of a virgin was also predicted by Isaiah when he wrote,

> *'The Lord himself will give you a sign: The virgin will be with child and will give birth to a son, and will call him Immanuel.'*   (Isaiah 7:14, NIV)

The circumstances surrounding His birth were quite outstanding too. We have angels appearing to shepherds heralding His coming with the message,

> *'Be not afraid; for behold, I bring you good news of a great Joy which will come to all the people; for to you is born this day in the city of David a Saviour, who is Christ the Lord.'* (Luke 2:10 & 11)

Then we have the wise men who were prepared to leave their homeland and follow a moving star which led them to the very place where Christ would be found.

Even the small town where Jesus was to be born was predicted by the prophet Micah when he wrote,

> *'But you, O Bethlehem Eph'rathah, who are little to be among the clans of Judah, from you shall come forth for me one who is to be ruler in Israel, whose origin is from old, from ancient days.'* (Micah 5:2)

Also the purpose of His coming and involvement in people's problems was foretold;

> *'The Spirit of the Lord God is upon me, because the Lord has anointed me to bring good tidings to the afflicted; he has sent me to bind up the brokenhearted, to proclaim liberty to the captives, and the opening of the prison to those who are bound...'* (Isaiah 61:1)

Secondly – *His Unique Life*

As Jesus grew up, His daily living was sinless. He had the strictest moral teaching of any other teacher in history but the notable thing was, He practised what He preached. This was certainly no ordinary man. The testimony that scripture gives to His life is quite startling. It says,

> *'He is the image of the invisible God, the first-born of all creation; for in him all things were created, in heaven and on earth, visible and invisible, whether thrones or dominions or principalities or authorities –*

*all things were created through him and for him. He is
before all things, and in him all things hold together.'*
(Colossians 1:15–17)

Just a few verses further on we also read,

>*'For in him all the fulness of God was pleased to dwell.'*
> (Colossians 1:19)

Throughout His life His words made a deep impression on people. In fact Jesus said some unique things about Himself which caused others to exclaim,

>*'. . . no man ever spoke like this man.'*   (John 7:46)

Some of these remarkable statements about His life were,

>*'Before Abraham was, I AM.'*   (John 8:58)

>*'I and the Father are one.'*   (John 10:30)

>*'I am the door; if any one enters by me, he shall be
saved . . . '*   (John 10:9)

>*'I am the resurrection and the life; he who believes in
me, though he die, yet shall he live.'*   (John 11:25)

Jesus continually used the phrase *'I AM'* – the Hebrew word meaning 'Yahweh'. For the Jew that was the name of God and therefore very sacred. He was deliberately using God's name.

What really caused a stir was when Jesus said,

>*'I am the way, and the truth, and the life; no one comes
to the Father, but by me.'*   (John 14:6)

It's the little word **'the'** that provoked such a reaction then, and still does today. This is an exclusive word saying, I am the only way, and means that you need no one else. No other person can save you. Peter emphasised this same unique statement when he preached,

> *'There is salvation in no one else, for there is no other name under heaven given among men by which we must be saved.'* (Acts 4:12)

The most outstanding thing about the life of Jesus was that it was full of miracles. Everywhere He went supernatural power was evident, turning people to God and giving confirmation to the words He spoke. He turned water into wine, healed the sick, raised the dead, drove out demons, commanded a fierce storm to be still, walked on water, and fed five thousand people with just a few loaves and fishes.

Thirdly – *His Unique Death*
Jesus was not a helpless victim. He not only predicted His own death, He also planned the time, the place and the manner that He would die. He was fully aware of what was going to happen. In fact Jesus said,

> *'I lay down my life, that I may take it again. No one takes it from me, but I lay it down of my own accord. I have power to lay it down, and I have power to take it again...'* (John 10:17 & 18)

When Jesus was explaining His death to the disciples He said,

> *'... the Son of man came not to be served but to serve, and to give his life as a ransom for many.'*
> (Matthew 20:28)

A ransom is the price paid to release someone from their kidnappers. This was the divine purpose and plan of God; to set mankind free from the captivity of sin and bondage to Satan. Amazingly the Bible tells us that this was an event planned from the beginning of time. It speaks of Jesus as,

> '... the Lamb that was slain from the creation of the world.'
> (Revelation 13:8, NIV)

The death of Jesus was the fulfilment of Isaiah's prophecy given hundreds of years before it took place. Here we read,

> 'He was despised and rejected by men; a man of sorrows, and acquainted with grief; and as one from whom men hide their faces he was despised, and we esteemed him not. Surely he has borne our griefs and carried our sorrows; yet we esteemed him stricken, smitten by God, and afflicted. But he was wounded for our transgressions, he was bruised for our iniquities; upon him was the chastisement that made us whole, and with his stripes we are healed.'
> (Isaiah 53:3–5)

The charge brought against Jesus that led to His crucifixion was blasphemy, for He declared himself to be the Son of God and the Mosaic Law decreed that blasphemy deserved death. This charge was put to Him very directly by the high priest when he said, 'Are you the Christ the Son of the Blessed?' and Jesus answered, 'I AM' (Mark 14:61 & 62).

The most outstanding fact about His death was that those who were the closest observers of all He did and said, felt He was innocent. First of all we have Pilate who declared, 'I find **no crime** in him' (John 18:38b). Then there was Pilate's wife who sent a message to her husband saying, 'Have nothing to do with that **righteous** man, for I have suffered much over him today in a dream' (Matthew 27:19). Also one of the two thieves dying right beside the Lord, rebuked his fellow criminal who was jeering at Jesus. Telling him to keep silent he said, '... we are receiving the due reward of our deeds; but **this man has done nothing wrong**'

(Luke 23:41). The Roman centurion guarding the cross up until the point of Christ's death, having heard and observed everything concluded, *'Truly this was the Son of God!'* (Matthew 27:54b). Even Judas after his betrayal of the Lord cried out in anguish, *'I have sinned in betraying innocent blood.'* (Matthew 27:4).

There is a great significance in that *'innocent blood'* for us today. The Bible says,

> *'The blood of Jesus God's Son cleanses us from all sin.'*
> (1 John 1:7b)

Jesus died, not for His own sins, but to become our substitute, to bear in His own body the sin, grief and sickness of mankind. When John the Baptist first met Jesus his reaction was to declare,

> *'Behold, the Lamb of God, who takes away the sin of the world!'* (John 1:29b)

In Jewish culture, because they understood that their sins could be atoned for by sacrificing a lamb, they would have immediately understood the relevance of John's statement.

When Jesus died on the cross He didn't cry out, *'I am finished,'* but in triumph said, *'It is finished!'* The divine purpose of God had been accomplished through Christ. In His death, Jesus triumphed over all evil, bore the penalty for sin and reconciled man back to God. As that cry rang out, the veil inside the Jewish temple, which separated man from God's presence was torn in two, straight down the middle, from top to bottom. Normally only the High Priest could go through this veil into the Holy presence of God once a year, to offer a sacrifice on behalf of the people. But when Jesus died, miraculously the veil, which was the thickness of a man's hand, was rent in two. Not one thread was left to prevent man's approach to God. Access was made possible for all by the death of Christ.

The Scriptures speak of this in saying,

'...since we have confidence to enter the sanctuary by the blood of Jesus, by the new and living way which he opened for us through the curtain, that is, through his flesh, and since we have a great priest over the house of God, let us draw near with a true heart in full assurance of faith, with our hearts sprinkled clean from an evil conscience and our bodies washed with pure water.'

(Hebrews 10:19–22)

Fourthly – *His Unique Resurrection*

It has been said, there is a thousand times more evidence that Jesus rose from the dead than for Julius Caesar's invasion of England!

Some years ago a young legal scholar called Frank Morison, set out to write a book on the last seven days of Jesus. His intention was to disprove the resurrection story. Having carefully studied all the evidence he was finally convinced of its truth and wonderfully converted. Later he wrote his classic book entitled, *Who Moved the Stone?* In doing so Frank Morison concluded,

'There certainly is a deep and profoundly historical basis for that much disputed sentence in the Apostles' Creed, – "The third day He rose again from the dead."'

Robert Lowry the hymn writer, in describing the resurrection of Christ, put it so well when he penned the words;

'Death could not hold its prey, Jesus my saviour,
He tore the bars away, Jesus my Lord.
Up from the grave He arose
With a mighty triumph over His foes.
He arose a victor from the dark domain and
He lives forever with His saints to reign.
He arose, He arose, Hallelujah Christ arose!'

On several occasions in the gospels, Jesus predicted His own resurrection. He made this clear to His disciples when He said,

> '... the Son of man will be delivered to the chief priests and scribes, and they will condemn him to death, and deliver him to the Gentiles to be mocked and scourged and crucified, and he will be raised on the third day.'
>
> (Matthew 20:18–19)

This is what makes the Christian faith so distinctive from all other religions and why Jesus stands apart from every other religious leader. It is for this reason that compromise regarding the uniqueness of Christ is totally impossible. You can go to the burial place of Buddha, Mohammed, any Hindu Guru or great philosopher and you will still find their bones. The tomb of Jesus though is empty, because He is risen!

One of the greatest evidences of the resurrection is without doubt a changed life! The risen Christ meets people in their problems and transforms them completely. This was so when Jesus appeared to His anxious, fearful disciples. All their insecurity was changed into an outstanding boldness. They were prepared to go out preaching the gospel even when faced with death because of their conviction that Jesus was alive!

As far as Peter was concerned the resurrection dramatically changed all the guilt and failure that he felt following his denial of the Lord. So much so that he was able to stand and preach about people's need to repent of their sin and the urgency to turn to Christ as Saviour. He proclaimed Jesus with uncompromising confidence before many thousands on the day of Pentecost, resulting in over three thousand committing their lives to the Lord.

Then there was doubting Thomas, who was full of scepticism when his friends reported that they had seen Jesus alive. In fact he refused to accept it unless he could see some tangible evidence. However, when the Lord appeared to him, his life was so changed that he exclaimed, *'My Lord and my God!'* (John 20:28). Doubting Thomas was the first person ever to call Jesus 'God'.

The most outstanding conversion that the resurrection brought was to Saul of Tarsus. All his religious bigotry and prejudice was totally changed as he met the risen Christ on the Damascus road. His life was so transformed that he was converted from being a Christ hater to a Christ proclaimer. Saul was changed from a murderer to a missionary! When confronted with the truth of the resurrection, lives are never the same again!

It is because of the uniqueness of who Jesus is that people can have confidence to bring the problems of their lives to Him. His words in Matthew 11:28 & 29 are as relevant today as they were when they were first spoken.

> *'Come to me all who labour and are heavy laden, and I will give you rest. Take my yoke upon you, and learn of me: for I am gentle and lowly in heart, and you will find rest for your souls.'*

In responding by faith to that personal invitation people can experience the miracle of not only a new start in life but a new life to start!

Chapter 3

Tackling Anxiety and Worry

One of the most famous escape artists of all time was Harry Houdini who lived from 1874–1926. Born in Budapest, he later emigrated to America where he eventually earned an international reputation. Among his many sensational acts was a feat that he used to enjoy with the help of the police. For this, officers would lock him up in a cell and as they walked away, he would follow them, already loose within seconds. Time and again he would do this with seemingly very little effort at all, except once. On this occasion half an hour went by and he was still fumbling over the lock until a policeman came up to the cell smiling, and simply pushed open the door! Houdini was fooled into trying to unlock what was already open!

Millions today are sweating, trying to get out of their various problems. They join new cults or old heathen religions, hear new theories or go to psychiatrists searching for help. The fact is though, because of the saving work of Christ Jesus, His cry from the cross, *'It is finished,'* means just what it says. Through Jesus Christ alone, all has been accomplished to release us from every bondage. The prison door has already been unlocked and liberty is now possible to all who believe. What a wonderful assurance this is as we face the numerous pressures that confront us today.

In looking at the subject of 'Tackling Anxiety and Worry' the Bible's teaching is relevant and practical. Let us first be clear though about what we are actually referring to. It is not the 'flash thought' of anxiety which affects us all that we are looking at. Nor is it the emotion which, when facing danger, causes adrenalin to flow, enabling us to be more alert. Neither are we talking about a concern for someone, or a situation, that has a positive effect upon us and motivates us to prayer. What we can know freedom from however, is the negative result anxiety has on our lives as it eats away at our peace, destroying our joy and causing us to hold on to situations, worrying. God wants us to know victory over anything that spoils the quality of our lives and stops us fulfilling our full potential.

While speaking at a Pentecostal Church in Spennymoor, Co. Durham recently, a man shared that on my previous visit to the church, over two years ago, he had responded for prayer. His problem was that he had been struggling with stress. Not only had his health suffered because of this, but also his ability to cope had been affected because of panic attacks. As he was telling me this, his face was so radiant that it was obvious God had worked a miracle. He said, 'Shortly after you prayed I immediately felt better and from that time to this, I've not had a single panic attack!'

The Extent of the Problem

Anxiety is one of the most prevailing characteristics of 20th century living. In this modern day and age in which we live, with all our sophistication, technology and materialism the problem is greater than it has ever been. We read in the scriptures that,

> *'In the last days there will come times of stress'*
> (2 Timothy 3:1)

and also of,

44

'Men's hearts failing them for fear ...'

(Luke 21:26, AV)

Increasingly the pressure and problems of life are beginning to take their toll. A leading psychologist by the name
of Rollo May has called anxiety, 'One of the most urgent
problems of our day.' It has been termed, 'The official
emotion of our age,' 'The basis of all neurosis,' and 'The
most pervasive psychological phenomenon of our time.'

This word 'anxiety', encompasses a wide range of different feelings like, uneasiness, tension, nervousness, worry,
fear, stress and even dread. We can all identify with such
experiences in varying degrees, because in some measure
they 'stalk' each of us from birth to the grave! Anxiety is
found in every walk of life no matter who we are. Whether
we are male or female, black or white, rich or poor,
healthy or sick, famous or unknown, the problem is common to everyone.

Some people though, seem to worry all the time about
anything and everything. If there's nothing for them to
worry about then they're anxious because there's nothing
to worry about! Just like a lady that I met after speaking at
a church in Essex. She came up to me for prayer with the
words, 'I'm a born worrier, my mother was a born worrier
and I am too!' Fortunately most people are not like this.
The majority of people only get anxious and start to worry
when things go wrong. For example, when there are
difficulties in their marriage, or a crisis in the family, perhaps conflict at work or uncertainty about the future,
maybe financial pressure or the threat of sickness. It's
when problems begin knocking on our door that anxiety
comes in.

The reason why what we're talking about is so serious is
because not only does anxiety affect every single person, it
also can have consequences in every area of our lives. Its
influence can make an impact upon us **physically**, **emotionally** and **spiritually**.

Physically

Any doctor will tell you of the clear connection between anxiety and a number of different physical conditions. Not just the obvious symptoms of, 'butterflies in the stomach', shortness of breath, loss of appetite, or the inability to sleep. Prolonged anxiety can also disrupt our physical well being. According to an article in the *British Medical Journal*, 'There is not an organ or tissue in the human body that is not influenced by the attitude of mind and spirit.' What goes on in one part of our being is able to transfer itself to other areas of our body and so we can find ourselves physically sick. A nerve specialist by the name of Dr Frank Hutchins has stated, '70% of all the medical cases I see need new spiritual and mental attitudes for healthy living.' Isn't it interesting that the 'experts' are just beginning to tell us what the Bible has always taught? The word of God says,

> '*A tranquil mind gives life to the flesh . . .*'
>
> (Proverbs 14:30)

Emotionally

Each one of us is indeed wonderfully made. We are all amazing 'works of art'. This is especially so when we consider our emotions which are extremely complex and only fully understood by God. When anxiety begins to influence the emotions then all sorts of complicated and unpredictable behaviour can result.

After speaking at an evening meeting in Staffordshire, the host I was staying with asked for prayer. He was regularly troubled by the fear of enclosed spaces and would often wake up in the night having nightmares in which he was choking and unable to breathe. The anxiety this caused would be so bad that he would have to get up and go out into the middle of the street until the stress passed. Even during the day he would have panic attacks in the house and feel that the walls were closing in on him. The doctors could do nothing to help his situation. After prayer that night though, he said he'd had no problems sleeping and believed God had set him free. I know this man personally, and two years later he is still free!

One elderly Christian man from Stoke shared with me that for over sixty years, since the age of six, he'd had a fear of water. This was the result of being thrown in the deep end of a swimming pool by a gang of youths and nearly drowning! The fear was so strong that it made him nervously anxious about any contact with water. He literally couldn't have a bath or even a shower, but had to be so careful about the way he applied water to his body. This was his emotional prison for more than sixty years. As strong as these fears were, the Lord worked a tremendous miracle in his life and set him completely free from all his anxiety. After his release he was even able to be baptised by full immersion in water as evidence of that miracle!

As these testimonies show, anxiety can grip a person's emotions throwing them into an irrational panic. This same effect can be found also in the Bible. For example, who would have thought Elijah, that man of faith, could ever have been seized by such anxiety? This is what happened though, shortly after that tremendous victory on Mount Carmel. He became so anxious when he heard of the Queen's anger and threat against him that he ran away in fear to hide. His worrying even dragged him down to the point where he wanted God to take away his life! (1 Kings 19:1–4)

We see also Peter, that lion of a man, one moment declaring he would follow Jesus, even to the grave and never deny Him, regardless of the cost. Yet when a young servant girl accused him of being one of Christ's disciples, anxiety caused him to panic so greatly that with oaths and curses he denied ever knowing the Lord (Matthew 26:69–74).

Spiritually

The development of a person's ability and effectiveness

can be dramatically hindered by anxiety. An example of this is seen with the army of Israel and illustrates how people can be paralysed spiritually from knowing victory over the enemy. These mighty warriors who should have been marching forward, reclaiming the land promised to them by God were paralysed by the mention of one name – **Goliath!** Their fear of him was so great that they allowed this giant to taunt and mock them. None of God's army dared step forward to do anything about it (1 Samuel 17:23–24).

Our potential can also be locked up and we can be spiritually imprisoned by anxiety, just like the disciples were, after the death of Jesus. The Bible says of them that they were behind locked doors for fear of the Jews (John 20:19). These people, who had been chosen by the Lord to turn the world upside down, were deeply worried that the same fate which had met Jesus, might befall them too. Because of this they remained contained behind a door, bound by their fears.

Fear of the unknown has often kept man from moving forward. In the early Middle Ages for example, European sailors would not sail very far south. They believed that the middle of the earth was ringed with fire, because the further south they travelled the hotter it became. The same kind of fear kept people from exploring the Atlantic Ocean. A chart that was drawn sometime in the Middle Ages has a painting of a ship turning back in the Mediterranean Sea from the Straits of Gibraltar. Above it appears the Latin phrase *'Ne Plus Ultra'*, which means 'Nothing more beyond'. Fear of the unknown kept explorers from crossing the Atlantic until Columbus decided to break out and test the horizon.

There are Christians today who are either paralysed from living in victory or restricted from launching out in faith and it all starts with anxious fear. This is why God's word tells us,

'The fear of man lays a snare . . . '   (Proverbs 29:25)

Fear of failure, rejection, being misunderstood, making a fool of ourselves and worrying about what others might think, is a difficulty to so many.

The Bible however gives us good cause for hope. One of the most common phrases Jesus spoke throughout His ministry was, *'Fear not,'* or, *'Do not be afraid.'* In fact we read this 365 times in the scriptures – one for every day of the year! What a wonderful prospect, we can wake up each morning and face the pressures of every day knowing that we need not be afraid. We can be the most positive and secure people on the face of this earth! This is why God's word says,

> *'Thou dost keep him in perfect peace, whose mind is stayed on thee . . .'* (Isaiah 26:3)

The key is not 'religion', but a close meaningful relationship with Christ that is expressed by living in obedience to His word. The word of Christ in relation to anxiety and worry is,

> *'Let not your heart be troubled . . .'* (John 14:1)

As we dwell upon this instruction it means, we don't have to let our hearts be troubled nor need we allow our mind to be tormented. This verse tells us there is something we can do about the situation! Some people live as though anxiety and worry is part of their lot in life, an unfortunate cross that they have to bear. Jesus however says, *'Do not let your heart be troubled.'*

Although this problem is common and has far reaching effects throughout people's lives, the practical steps in God's word are powerful. The words of Christ as He speaks to His anxious disciples show us God's answer. In looking at Matthew 6:25–34, we are given five steps to enable us to overcome anxiety and worry.

49

1. Renew Your Thinking

Our lives must be lived according to scriptural principles. We need to look at every situation (especially the things that worry us), from a spiritual perspective. This is what the disciples failed to do. The passage in Matthew chapter 6 shows us that in all their anxiety there was not a spiritual perspective in sight! They were worried about food, drink, clothing and the cares of tomorrow. Their whole thought-life was set entirely upon material and natural things. Because of this Jesus asks one simple question to begin to renew their thinking. He raises their minds to a new dimension as He says,

> 'Is not life more than food, and the body more than clothing?'
> (Matthew 6:25b)

Jesus was getting them to start thinking on a completely different plane and to view their situation with 'spiritual eyes'.

The battleground really is our thought life and if the enemy can build a stronghold there, he literally can begin to manipulate and control our entire living. If we are not disciplined in this area then a stronghold can easily be built by Satan. He accomplishes this by sowing doubts, whispering lies and suggesting those things that are going to go wrong. As we allow what is negative and contrary to God's word to settle in our minds we begin to act accordingly. Whatever our mind is focused upon will certainly have a controlling influence in our lives.

According to psychologists, we speak to ourselves (not out loud), at the rate of 1300 words a minute. Many people go through life convincing themselves they're going to fail, they're incompetent, not good looking or unable to cope etc. Therefore if negative thoughts try to stay in our mind we need to learn how to argue with them on the basis of scripture. Anxious, irrational and unscriptural thoughts must succumb to the authority of God's word. This is why the Bible teaches that we are to,

50

> '...take captive every thought to make it obedient to Christ.' (2 Corinthians 10:5b, NIV)

If we don't take anxious thoughts captive then we become a prisoner to them. We see the potential again of our minds affecting our lives when the apostle Paul says,

> 'Do not be conformed to this world but be transformed by the renewal of your mind...' (Romans 12:2)

The best prescription for anxiety and worry is received not from the doctor's surgery but directly from the scriptures. In Philippians 4:6 & 7 Paul writes from a place of potential fear; not the comfort of a palace but the coldness of a prison cell! Yet in spite of these circumstances he says,

> 'Have no anxiety about anything, but in everything by prayer and supplication with thanksgiving let your requests be made known to God. And the peace of God, which passes all understanding, will keep your hearts and your **minds** in Christ Jesus.'

The clear strategy for victory here is – **Prayer and Praise leads to Peace in any situation.** It works because when we are faced with difficulties and pressures but keep on praying to God and praising Him, what we are actually doing, is 'thinking spiritually'. This is a choice each of us has, in every problem we might face. It is expressed so well in the words,

> 'To set the mind on the flesh is death, but to set the mind on the Spirit is life and peace.' (Romans 8:6)

The only way we can renew our thinking and win the battle ground of the mind, is by accepting our responsibility to set our minds upon the word of God. As someone once said, 'Soak your mind in the scriptures until like cloth soaked in dye the two become inseparable and your thinking is permanently coloured by God's Word.'

2. Re-evaluate Your Priorities

So many come under unnecessary stress, quite simply because they have the wrong priorities in life. People live such busy lives today, pursuing their career and ambitions, wanting to improve themselves and their standard of living. All that is done might appear very impressive and have material benefits, but can result in being so busy that there is no time to come aside and wait on God. The inevitable outcome then will be a draining away of their strength and a weakening in their relationship with the Lord. We need to constantly re-assess the things that we spend our time and energy on. Unless we re-evaluate our priorities we could find ourselves 'entangled' in fruitless activity, missing God's will, doing things in our own ability and leaving the Lord out!

There was surely no one more active and consumed with good works than Jesus. Constant demands were also made upon His time as people clamoured for His attention. In spite of this He took care that the priorities of His life were God-centred. He said,

> *'For I have come down from heaven, not to do my own will, but the will of him who sent me.'*   (John 6:38)

Jesus made time to be sure His priorities were serving God's purpose, so much so that we read of Him,

> *'And in the morning, a great while before day, he rose and went out to a lonely place, and there he prayed.'*
> (Mark 1:35).

Again, in the busyness of His life we notice,

> *'In these days he went out to the mountain to pray; and all night he continued in prayer to God.'*   (Luke 6:12)

This was the important principle that Jesus taught His disciples in Matthew chapter 6. Confronting their anxiety about their material needs, Jesus instructed them,

> *'Seek first his Kingdom and his righteousness, and all these things shall be yours as well.'*   (Matthew 6:33)

We are not to be like others in the world who have the attitude of making sure they look after themselves. Nor do we need to be concerned about grabbing the things we feel are necessary for security, comfort and success. Our priority and passion should be a determination that God's purpose and will is central to our lives. God then promises to provide for us whatever we need. This principle is put in a similar way by the Psalmist when he says,

> *'Take delight in the Lord, and he will give you the desires of your heart.'*   (Psalm 37:4)

3. Recognise Your Value to God

One of the most common problems that people struggle with today is a feeling of low self-worth. We'll be looking at this area in greater detail in a later chapter on 'Overcoming Insecurity', but it is also the cause of a lot of anxiety in the lives of many people.

Each one of us is of immense value to God. We are unique individuals in His sight and of great worth. The Bible tells us how much we mean to Him when it says,

> *'. . . he will exalt over you with loud singing as on a day of festival.'*   (Zephaniah 3:17b)

When we are confident in His love, it brings an unshakeable security as we face the pressures and problems of the day. The effect and power of God's love is seen in the words of the apostle John,

> *'Perfect love drives out fear . . .'*   (1 John 4:18, NIV)

53

There is no room for fear when we are secure in God's love.

The problem is that too often we look around at other people and make comparisons. We observe their beauty, strength, personality, intellect, ability and possessions etc, then look at ourselves. This results in leaving us feeling inadequate and inferior, as though we don't quite measure up and there's something wrong with us. I would imagine we've all looked at ourselves in the mirror at least once and thought, 'If only I wasn't so fat,' or 'I wish I wasn't so thin.' 'If only I wasn't so tall or so short.' 'If only my nose wasn't so pointed!' How can we truly believe that God loves us and considers we are of great worth if we don't love and accept ourselves? The fact is God loves us just as we are and He has not made a mistake with anyone of us. A well known children's chorus expresses this so simply with the words,

> 'He gave me a heart, and He gave me a smile,
> He gave me Jesus and He made me His child and
> I just thank you Father for making me, me!'

Unless we can say those words, really meaning them, and come to accept ourselves, then we will constantly be troubled by anxiety.

This was precisely the problem that Jesus was dealing with in Matthew 6 in the lives of His worried disciples. They just did not recognise their unique worth to God. They couldn't appreciate how precious they were to Him. Because of this, Jesus spoke in a marvellous way to reassure and help them see God's love. Notice, that sandwiched in between His words, *'Look at the birds of the air'* (verse 26) and *'Consider the lilies of the field'* (verse 28), Jesus says, *'Are you not of more value than they?'* (verse 26b). The Lord was showing them that God was concerned to care for the birds and lilies. In the same way their Heavenly Father would certainly take care of His children, because they were of far greater value.

4. Realise Worry Changes Nothing

Jesus asks the question in Matthew 6:27

> *'And which of you by being anxious can add one cubit to his span of life?'*

The answer of course is, all the worry in the world will not change a single thing, so we might just as well stop worrying! Worry is like a rocking chair – it will give you something to do, but it won't get you anywhere! This fact is straight forward and obvious and yet, 'letting go' is something that seems so hard at times to do. More often than not when we've got a problem, we bring it to God and give the burden to Him as we pray in 'faith'. Then when we've finished praying, we take the burden back again and worry about it a bit more! The scripture says,

> *'Cast your burden on the Lord, and he will sustain you; he will never permit the righteous to be moved.'*
>
> (Psalm 55:22)

Lasting peace comes only when we have surrendered all to the Lord and are confident that He is for us. Knowing He hasn't forgotten us and He's aware of our problem enables us to truly let go of what we are holding on to.

Hudson Taylor, who was a missionary in China and founder of what is today known as the 'The Overseas Missionary Fellowship', gave this excellent advice:

> 'Let us give up our work, our plans, ourselves, our lives, our loved ones, our influence, our all, right into God's hand; and then, when we have given all over to Him, there will be nothing left for us to be troubled about.'

One other practical thing in helping us let go of our worries is to see that most anxiety is about the future:

those things that might go wrong and the problems that could occur. Rarely are they about the present, though worry does affect the present. As someone once said, 'You can't change the past, but you can ruin a perfectly good present by worrying about the future!' This is why Jesus said to His disciples,

> *'Therefore do not be anxious about tomorrow, for tomorrow will be anxious for itself. Let the day's own trouble be sufficient for the day.'* (Matthew 6:34)

In reality, **Today is the tomorrow you worried about yesterday!** When we look at it like this, we begin to see that what we were worrying about didn't turn out as bad as we thought it would; in fact many, if not all of our fears were never realised.

5. Renounce All Unbelief

This is an essential part of tackling the problem and must not be neglected. In seeking to overcome worry we should want to do so, not merely because of the distress it brings to us, but above all because it displeases the Lord. As we worry, we believe more in our problems than in God's promises. Therefore we need to ask God's forgiveness for doubting His Word and His love. When the Lord was speaking to His disciples about their anxiety, He put His finger right on the heart of the issue. Jesus said, '... *O men of little faith*' (Matthew 6:30b). It was doubt that had opened the door to worry and anxiety and the only way to close that door is through confessing the sin of unbelief and renouncing it. One definition of worry is, 'Unholy Meditation'. When we look at the problem in that light, it helps us recognise the seriousness of the situation.

As part of our willingness to renounce unbelief, it is important that we make a firm decision to quit worrying. The strength needed for this will be given to us, as we commit ourselves to feeding upon those things which will build our faith and weaken our doubts. The spiritual diet for healthy, anxious free living that we need to feed on is spoken of by Paul;

> *'Whatever is true, whatever is honourable, whatever is just, whatever is pure, whatever is lovely, whatever is gracious, if there is any excellence, if there is anything worthy of praise, think about these. What you have learned and received and heard and seen in me, do; and the God of Peace will be with you.'*

(Philippians 4:8–9)

It is when we take responsibility for filling our minds with truth and righteousness, that God will take responsibility for filling it with peace!

Chapter 4

Letting Go of Resentment

It is said of the gifted artist Leonardo da Vinci, that just before starting his painting of 'The Last Supper', he had a nasty argument with a fellow artist. Leonardo felt so bitter towards his rival, that he determined to paint his enemy as the face of Judas. By picturing him as the betrayer of Jesus, he would take revenge on the man and make his face the object of scorn to all who viewed the painting. Judas was one of the first that da Vinci finished, and everyone could easily recognise him as the painter with whom he had quarrelled. But when Leonardo da Vinci began to paint the face of Jesus, he could make no progress at all. Something seemed to be hindering his best efforts. He finally came to the realisation that the frustration he was experiencing was due to his continual hatred of his enemy. Leonardo immediately painted out the face of Judas and began again on the face of Christ, this time with the success that the years have come to acclaim.

One of the great struggles that people have today is in this area of resentment towards others. Not many have the skin of a rhinoceros! Generally speaking we are not 'thick skinned'. We're easily hurt, bruised and offended, but the instruction of the Bible could not be more clear. It says,

> 'Be angry but do not sin; do not let the sun go down on your anger, and give no opportunity to the devil . . . Let

*all bitterness and wrath and anger and clamour and
slander be put away from you, with all malice, and be
kind to one another, tenderhearted, forgiving one
another, as God in Christ forgave you.'*

(Ephesians 4:26–32)

God is a Unilateralist!

No this isn't the start of a political speech, or the latest
statement from the CND movement on nuclear disarma-
ment! It is though, a powerful biblical truth that when
applied to our lives, pulls down the devil's strongholds
within our attitudes and can disarm even our fiercest
enemy. Unilateral, means, a 'one sided action' and in
terms of forgiveness, is an attitude that takes the initia-
tive. It is a love which flows from the person who has been
hurt without waiting for the offender to come and apolo-
gise or ask to be forgiven. This is why God's word says in
Ephesians 4:32b, *'... forgiving one another, as God in
Christ forgave you.'* God forgave us unilaterally. It was
while we were indifferent to His love and hostile to His
law that Christ died for our sins.

As we look at the life of Jesus we see this same principle.
No one ever came to Him and specifically asked to be forgiven; even so, forgiveness flowed from His heart to
others. The paralytic man on the stretcher who was
brought to the Lord, came looking for healing, but the
first thing Jesus said to him was, *'Take heart, my son; your
sins are forgiven'* (Matthew 9:2b). Also the woman who
knelt before Jesus weeping, washing His feet with her tears
and drying them with her hair, heard the words, *'Your sins
are forgiven'* (Luke 7:48b). This Jesus said, although she
had not sought any forgiveness.

Peter asks the question,

> *'Lord, how often shall my brother sin against me, and I
> forgive him? As many as seven times?' Jesus said to*

60

*him, 'I do not say to you seven times, but seventy times
seven.'*   (Matthew 18:21 & 22)

The Lord was not demonstrating here that we should ever
put a limit on how many times we are prepared to forgive,
but that we should go on and on forgiving. The most grip-
ping example of unilateral forgiveness that doesn't draw
the line, is seen at the crucifixion of Jesus, as He hangs
upon the cross. Having been rejected, falsely accused,
abused, humiliated and nailed to a wooden gibbet, Jesus
cries out to God, *'Father, forgive them; for they know not
what they do'* (Luke 23:34).

The marvellous thing about God's love is the way in
which it is constant and unconditional. It is not determined by our attitude to Him. He loves us and there's
nothing we can do that will ever change that. Whether we
believe it, feel it, understand, or deserve it, He will still go
on loving us. The Bible says,

*'The steadfast love of the Lord never ceases, his mer-
cies never come to an end.'*   (Lamentations 3:22)

It is a stubborn love that is consistent, selfless and unyield-
ing. Having God's supernatural love in our hearts enables
us to forgive and let go of all resentment, and this is how
He wants us to relate to other people.

The name of Gordon Wilson came to the attention of
the nation on Remembrance Sunday in November 1987.
He was an elderly man who tragically lost his daughter,
Marie, a young nurse in her 20s. Her life was cruelly
snatched away through a terrorist bombing at Enniskellen
in Ireland. After this awful incident, the response of her
father was headline news in the national press. His words
were, **'I Forgive the Terrorists.'** He explained that the only
way he could say this was because of his Christian faith
and the knowledge that resentment and bitterness would
only destroy him. Gordon Wilson is now involved as a
political spokesman in Ireland. He has even sat down with

those who murdered his daughter trying to bring peace for others to that land divided by hatred.

This expression of unilateral forgiveness can be a powerful means of making an impact on others, as they are challenged by the love of God. Primarily though, it is to keep our lives from getting all bound up with bitterness and resentment. It doesn't absolve those who have offended against us of responsibility. They should still seek forgiveness and put the matter right, but that's between them and God. What we are talking about here, is keeping our life and attitude right before the Lord.

The Network of Relationships

Resentment is common in the network of relationships, especially with people that we're closest to; those we see most frequently. We don't show bitterness towards the postman, because he only calls twice a day! It is with those we know well that we can have the greatest problems. For example: (a) in family relationships – between husband and wife, brother and sister, children and parents, in-laws etc.; (b) in the area of our church life, perhaps between a pastor and his congregation or between the members themselves; (c) in our place of work with colleagues or employers, and also of course with our neighbours whom we live beside, day in and day out.

Resentment comes into the network of these contacts in so many different ways. It could result from incidents that are quite recent, or perhaps something that goes back many years. For some people it's the sting of criticism that they've felt; for others, broken promises, or the feeling of being taken for granted and not appreciated; perhaps being let down, misjudged or misunderstood; maybe an off-hand comment, a flippant remark or some thoughtless action. Often resentment begins with something quite small that just irritates but develops into a greater problem. In other situations it really is a major issue that, but for the grace of God, would be impossible to forgive.

I remember last year speaking at a meeting in Kent when a man came into the church and sat on the back row. As I spoke about the importance of forgiveness, I could see he was deeply moved. When the invitation was made for people to respond, he came out along with others. This man was full of bitterness towards his wife who was suspected of murdering his two year old child. Also there was deep resentment towards the social services for the way he felt they had handled the situation. In hearing that night about the forgiveness of Christ for his sins, he said he wanted to let go of his anger and live in the power of forgiveness himself.

The Prison of Resentment

This is exactly what resentment becomes in a person's life; something that has the power to imprison. Ephesians 4:27 tells us to, *'give no opportunity to the devil.'* Through unforgiveness we allow ground to be given to evil spirits in our life and as a result we become bound by what we hold on to. One of the most common Greek words for forgiveness means 'to release', or 'let go' and this is essential if we are to find freedom from the power of resentment.

An interesting illustration that clarifies this point, is told of one of the ways South American monkey hunters catch their prey. They do this by getting a large fruit and making a small hole in it, just big enough for the monkey's hand to fit in. Then having hollowed it out inside and filled it with nuts, they strap it to the branch of a tree. As the monkey comes swinging through the trees and sees this, he squeezes his hand into the hole and grabs a fist full of the nuts. Then he tries to take his hand out but finds himself stuck! The foolish monkey hasn't got the sense to let go of the nuts and slip his hand back out, so refusing to let them go makes him a prisoner! He is bound by what he holds on to!

We not only restrict ourselves through resentment, we also put shackles on God! The only thing that can stop

His forgiveness flowing to us is when we withhold the same from someone else. If we don't forgive, then God's hands are tied and we cut ourselves off from His forgiveness. This is what Jesus taught when He said,

> *'If you do not forgive men their trespasses, neither will your Father forgive your trespasses.'* (Matthew 6:15)

John Wesley once met a man burning with resentment towards someone who had hurt him. The man full of bitterness said, 'I'll never forgive that person for what they've done to me!' John Wesley's reply was, 'You'd better pray then, that you never sin!' We remain in an unforgiven state if we have unforgiveness towards anyone, no matter what they have done to us. One lady that came to me for help after a meeting, had held on to resentment against her mother for over ten years! Not until she was willing to let the issue go did she find freedom herself.

Jesus taught that 'unforgiveness' brings us into a dark prison of torment (Matthew 18:23–35). It will cloud our vision of the Lord, hinder our faith and drain power from our prayers. Our spiritual relationship with God is seriously damaged if we do not forgive from our hearts.

On the 6th March 1986 Jill Saward, a vicar's daughter, age 21, was brutally attacked by three men and viciously raped. This took place at her home in Ealing, London. During a television documentary about the incident, she spoke of what happened shortly after that traumatic event. While in a church service, still struggling to come to terms with everything, she was quietly saying 'The Lord's Prayer'. The words, *'Forgive us our trespasses as we forgive those who trespass against us'* came to her in a new light. It was at this point, that she realised if she was to receive God's forgiveness in her life, then she had to forgive even her rapists. The interviewer listening to her story, gently asked the question, 'Is this forgiveness an intellectual thing, just coming from your head, or something deeper?' Jill replied, 'No, because of my Christian faith and what

Jesus has done for me, I can forgive those rapists from my heart!'

The Poison of Resentment

'Unforgiveness' will do more than affect us spiritually, it will pollute our whole lives. The poison of resentment and bitterness soon spreads, eating away at us, poisoning our thoughts and feelings. It colours the way we view people and comes out in our reactions and the things we say. Even when we don't notice it, it's there deep down in our emotions, smouldering away like a great volcano about to erupt at any time!

The poison of resentment is so powerful that just as in the previous chapter we spoke of anxiety and stress affecting our physical health, resentment can do so as well. The more I'm involved in ministry, the more convinced I've become about this fact. Certainly not all, but much of people's ill health is a result of inner, emotional conflicts. Doctors tell us that 75–80% of all illness is rooted in the emotions – 'psychosomatic'. This doesn't mean that a person's ailment is all in their head, that they just 'think' they're sick. There is actually a physical problem, but its origin is rooted in the emotions. Some disease today is a result of 'dis–ease' within the emotions. The Bible makes this very clear when it says,

> *'A calm and undisturbed mind and heart are the life and health of the body, but envy, jealousy and wrath are as rottenness of the bones.'*　　(Proverbs 14:30, Amp)

One Christian doctor has said, 'We are all allergic to wrong attitudes just like some people are allergic to shrimps or green peppers – it makes them sick. We are as God's creation, allergic to bitter, harsh, judgemental and unforgiving attitudes. They disrupt the body, soul and spirit and affect the way we feel.'

Dr S.I. McMillen says in his excellent book, *None of*

These Diseases, that ulcerative colitis, toxic goitres and high blood pressure are a few of the scores of diseases caused by bitterness. When we become resentful our pituitary, adrenal, thyroid and other glands give forth certain hormones, which cause disease in the body.

I remember some years ago talking to a Christian doctor from Colchester, after speaking at a conference there. As we sat together at the meal table, I asked him how he felt about the likelihood of our physical health being affected by such things. His response was immediate. He said, 'I've no doubt at all that a lot of people suffer physical symptoms because of unrighteous attitudes.' Then he proceeded to list some of the conditions that could well be affected by conflict in the emotions, making very clear though, that not in every case could you automatically assume the problem was emotional. He spoke of things like migraine, colitis, ulcers, eczema, high blood pressure and rheumatoid arthritis, to name but a few.

The Pattern of Resentment

There is a very specific pattern in the development of resentment. It is common to us all and one that most people will easily identify with.

Firstly – *The Inward Hurt*

This is where it begins, the 'ouch!' that we feel when we've been hurt or offended. That initial feeling of pain is often something that only ourselves and God know about. Even our partner or family member might be unaware of it. The inward hurt happens when we feel wronged or misjudged in some way. This is like a weed sown into our heart and if we don't deal with it right away, it soon becomes a root of bitterness. Either you kill the weed or the weed will kill you! This is why God's word says,

> '... *do not let the sun go down on your anger.*'
>
> (Ephesians 4:26b)

The application of this simple principle could dramatically change the quality of life today. If only it was put into practice right at the start of any disagreement the outcome would be so different. Just think how many marriages would be saved from the divorce courts. Consider the number of families that would be kept from breaking up. Imagine how many churches would avoid the splits and divisions that take place, if just this one instruction was heeded.

Secondly – *Re-run the Film*

This next stage is all too common. Having been hurt by a remark or incident, we then turn everything over and over again in our minds. Going through every detail we re-run each word that was spoken, the way we were treated and how we responded. Often as this takes place, what we are actually doing is trying to justify ourselves: seeking perhaps to justify what we said, how we felt and the way we reacted. In doing this, inevitably what happens is that everything gets distorted. What might have started off as something relatively small soon gets blown up out of all proportion in our minds. The more we 're-run the film' the less resemblance we have to what actually took place because it gets blurred and reinterpreted from our own perspectives.

Thirdly – *Self-pity Comes in*

'Everything's against me,' 'No-one understands,' 'Why does it always happen to me?' 'If only you knew how it feels!' It's here that the 'pity party' takes place to which we invite as many as possible to come and join in. The more people we tell about the event, the greater number we're likely to get on our side who can help reinforce our position. Self-pity in every circumstance, without exception, is always sin, because it centres on ourselves rather than upon Christ. We begin to dwell upon the problem rather than the answer and with every thought of self-pity we are turning our back on God. In this state, what we also do is contaminate those that are around us with our negative attitudes.

One other reason why self-pity is so dangerous is because of the way it prolongs the problem, causing resentment to grow rather than be dealt with. Imagine self-pity like a spade full of manure! What we are actually doing as we feel sorry for ourselves is putting more and more manure on the weed of bitterness. This makes it grow bigger, get stronger and enables its roots to go deeper into our lives.

Fourthly – *Seek Revenge*
This is usually the ultimate conclusion of resentment. We're angry, hurt and bitter inside and want to hit out in some way; if not physically then verbally, as we lash out with our tongues. This is why Ephesians 4 in the context of forgiveness says,

> *'Let no evil talk come out of your mouths.'*
> (Ephesians 4:29)

Also God's instructions are,

> *'Let all bitterness and wrath and anger and clamour and slander be put away from you, with all malice.'*
> (Ephesians 4:31)

Because we've been hurt then we want to get our own back. Perhaps simply by the manner in which we speak or the coldness of our attitude. Frequently this revenge can also take the form of character assassination of the one we have a grudge against, with things like criticism, gossip and half truths. Out of resentment we seek to turn other people against the person we feel has wronged us.

The Pathway to Freedom

The problem of resentment is an issue we all, to a greater

or lesser degree, need to deal with in our lives. In seeing that it can affect us emotionally, spiritually and physically, we can be encouraged that there is a path which leads to freedom. Let us consider four steps that bring us to this place of release.

1. Confession

Regardless of what people have done to us and in spite of how greatly we might feel hurt, resentment is sin. We are always in the wrong if we have resentment and 'unforgiveness' towards anyone. The Bible puts it in such terms that there is no excuse for avoiding our responsibility to forgive. It says,

> *'Whenever you stand praying, forgive, if you have any-*
> *thing against any one . . . '* (Mark 11:25)

In acknowledging our responsibility, we must first humble ourselves and confess our sin. Any wrong attitudes in our lives must first be dealt with. What the person did to us is no greater a sin than our harbouring resentment and withholding forgiveness from them. We need to see how much we have already been forgiven ourselves and let God empty out the stored up emotions. Some people have kept things bottled up for fifteen or twenty years. When they come to this place of confessing their sins and humbling themselves, it is like a great dam bursting, as their emotions are released.

There could well be occasions when we have caused offence to someone, but through pride think, 'I'm not going to make the first move, it's up to them!' This must be confessed also and followed through with action, because Jesus still places the responsibility on us to put things right. He says,

> *'So if you are offering your gift at the altar, and there*
> *remember that your brother has something against you,*
> *leave your gift there before the altar and go; first be*

69

reconciled to your brother, and then come and offer
your gift.' (Matthew 5:23–24)

2. Seek Healing

There will be a need to ask God to heal the memory of
what has been done or said. This doesn't mean you'll forget that it ever happened, a sort of 'heavenly amnesia'.
Some of the words and actions of others have been so
cruel that they will never completely be forgotten. However, as we ask the Lord to heal those memories we can
believe for the 'sting' to be taken away and gradually the
pain caused by the incident to begin to disappear.

There is some foolish teaching today that suggests when
we have forgiven, then automatically we can expect to forget. This is based on the false understanding, that once we
have confessed our sin to the Lord, then He can no longer
remember it, and we should do likewise. God would not be
God if He couldn't remember our sins and transgressions.
What His word says though, and what can help us with
our memory of being sinned against is,

'. . . I will forgive their iniquity, and I will remember
their sin no more.' (Jeremiah 31:34b)

This doesn't mean that God **'can't'** remember, but that
He **'won't'** remember. We too can deal with people's
offences against us in the same way. This statement by
God is a **choice**, a **promise** and a **commitment**. We need
also to take this same stand. We can choose not to bring
the painful thoughts before our memory any more. When
these try to creep back, we must remind ourselves of the
promise and commitment we've made before God. 'I have
chosen not to dwell on that memory and I commit myself
to rejecting it from my thought life!'

3. Be Positive in Prayer

To pray for God's love and compassion to be upon people
that have wronged us is a positive step that we can take. It

also changes our attitudes towards them. We'll find that it won't be possible to hold on to resentment if we're praying that they will be helped. It's not a case of thinking to ourselves, 'God says, *"Judgement is mine, I will repay,"* so I'll give the matter to Him and ask Him to **"zap"** them.' No, I believe the righteous attitude, that will be of most benefit to us, is to pray for God's goodness and mercy to be extended to them. This is why Jesus taught His disciples,

> *'love your enemies and pray for those who persecute you.'* (Matthew 5:44)

Even with His dying breath, Jesus responded to those who deserved nothing but judgement in this same way. He prayed God's mercy upon those who abused Him so greatly when He said, *'Father, forgive them; for they know not what they do'* (Luke 23:34).

We see this principle also in the suffering of Job. He had lost everything he possessed; even his children in a tragic accident. On top of all his grief, the final straw must have been when his friends let him down. Those who should have been a support, started to blame him for his own situation. They were suggesting that he was suffering because there was sin in his life. We can imagine how deep a wound that must have been to him and how easily he would have resented them for the insensitivity of their accusations. However, the turning point in Job's trials, when all his misfortune started to change, came as he let go of the resentment. It was then that restoration began! This is seen in that he prayed God's blessing upon those who had hurt and offended him. The scripture says,

> *'And the Lord restored the fortunes of Job, when he had prayed for his friends . . .'* (Job 42:10)

4. Wisdom for Reconciliation

Time needs to be taken to seek God carefully for wisdom about being reconciled with the person we have resented.

Sensitivity to what the Lord is saying, and the counsel of mature, spiritually minded people, will be of great benefit here. This is because it is not always helpful to actually tell the person who has offended us about our resentment. If they are not aware of our attitude towards them, it will not be wise in every case to go and tell them. Our intentions might well be good, but we could easily create a situation that is worse than the original. By off-loading how we've felt, we might find ourselves causing contention over the different perspectives on the situation. Also we could be loading guilt and mixed feelings upon the other person.

Where we have been openly resenting someone though, and there has been an obvious break in the relationship, then that is a different matter. If the issue is known both to us and the other party, it is important that we seek to be reconciled. It only takes a small key to open a large door and we have the key to the reconciliation so long as we are wise in how we use it. In some cases it might be best to write and express how we feel about the relationship being restored, in a letter. This way we can be clear and coherent. In other situations perhaps the Lord's direction will be to make a phone call right away to ask for forgiveness. Perhaps in other cases it would be appropriate to take that first step towards someone by visiting the person concerned. We could then express face to face our regret about the resentment and wrong attitudes we've had.

Maybe you're thinking right now, 'It's hard. You don't know what they've done: the things they've said and how I've been treated!' Well that's true, but God does, and we can always be sure of His help, if we seek to do what we know is right. The Lord will give us His grace, and who knows what amazing miracle could result?

This point is well illustrated by what happened some years ago in America. A woman giving her testimony in an interview on Christian television was sharing about her unhappy childhood. As a little girl of seven years, she had a mother with an uncontrollable temper who among other things, would grab her hair and knock her head against a wall. This was a regular occurrence and she would often get into such a rage that she'd just keep 'bashing' her daughter. Other times when the mother felt this rage coming on, she would lock her in a closet for a whole day at a time. One of the awful things the mother did when she really got angry was to stick her thumbs into the girl's eye sockets and push. Tragically, one day she pushed too hard and too long, which resulted in the little girl going completely blind.

The police and courts were immediately involved and the mother was sentenced to prison. The girl, aged eight by then, was put into a home for disabled children and a court order was made that mother and daughter should never see each other until the girl became an adult. She could then choose to see her mother if she wanted, but the mother could not see her until she was willing.

In that children's home, Christian groups would come in to sing to the handicapped children and one night the girl made a decision to receive Christ as Saviour. After her conversion all she wanted to do was to find her mother, but the authorities wouldn't allow it. Many years passed, and when eventually she left the home she went in search of her. On finding her mother she shared how Jesus had changed her life and then also had the joy of leading her to faith in Christ.

In this interview the woman said, 'As an adult now, I travel all over America giving my testimony. I'm still completely blind, but do you know who always comes along to carry my bags – my mother!' The interviewer asked how she had managed to forgive her saying, 'Some things you can put behind you and forget, but what she's done to you, you have to live with every day of your life, from the moment you wake up you're reminded of it!' The woman's reply was, 'When Jesus forgave me my sins, the first thing I wanted to do was forgive my mum!'

Chapter 5

Rising Up from Discouragement

In the hills of Eastern Tennessee a young lad walked across town to preach his first sermon. He'd felt God's call upon his life and all his friends and loved ones had packed the little country church to hear him preach. As he sat before the congregation the pastor introduced him. Rising to his feet, he opened his Bible read his text, bowed his head and prayed. Then he looked up to speak, and on seeing all those people, fear suddenly gripped him and he forgot his message. Not knowing what to do he sort of stuttered and stammered around for a moment and then sat back down in the chair. The pastor, caught totally unawares, tried to cover as best he could, but eventually had to close the meeting in prayer and dismiss the people.

Everybody went home, too embarrassed to say anything to the boy. No-one came by with an encouraging word. In the awkward silence they just left. Afterwards as he sat on the platform with his face in his hands, the janitor of the church, whose name was Moses, came walking down the centre of the aisle and stepped onto the platform. He said, 'It hurts doesn't it son?' The boy looked up with tears running down his cheeks and said, 'Moses, if the Lord will forgive me, I'll never try to preach another sermon as long as I live!' The janitor replied, 'Son you can't feel that way, here's what I want you to do. My wife's got a good dinner cooked at home, come back with me, you'll feel better when you've got something inside your stomach.'

Later that evening, after eating their meal, the two of them went outside, got a couple of old cane bottom chairs and leant them up against the house. Then they took out their Bibles and began to read and pray and talk about the Lord. After a while Moses said, 'Son I want you to kneel.' The young man got down on his knees and Moses put his hands on his head and prayed, 'Oh God, anoint this boy to preach the gospel. Send him to nations of the world with your healing power!'

The years passed by and the little country church outgrew its premises so they had to build a new building. When the dedication Sunday came they called on the Bishop who lived hundreds of miles away to speak at the service. The Bishop preached a tremendous message with the anointing of God on his life. As he got to the end of his sermon, he told the story about that young preacher and then said, 'Friends, I was that boy!' Then looking around the congregation he said, 'You all know me, I grew up here. After we've prayed and closed the service, I wonder whether anyone will raise their hand and take me home with them for lunch.' At that point everybody's hand immediately shot up!

The Bishop smiled and shook his head saying, 'Oh no ... Oh no.' Then he looked up to the balcony where old Moses was sitting, frail and white haired by now. 'Moses,' he called, 'I want you to come down here.' The old man made his way slowly down the steps, along to the front and walked up on the platform. As the Bishop put his arm around him he said, 'Moses, I want to go home with you today. I know your wife will have a good dinner cooked and after we've eaten I'd like us to go outside, get a couple of old cane bottom chairs and lean them up against the side of the house. We'll get out our Bibles, read together and talk about the Lord. Then Moses I'm going to get down on my knees and I'd like you to pray again for the blessing and anointing of God on my life!'

Moses had no idea how great a man that boy was to become. It was a sensitive heart, a listening ear and an encouraging word that enabled the young preacher to get up from the dust of discouragement and go on again for God.

The Causes of Discouragement

There are plenty of things to discourage us in life today, whether it's at work, in the church, at home or in our ministry. This is why the Bible says we are to,

> 'encourage one another daily, as long as it is called Today...'   (Hebrews 3:13, NIV)

Discouragement is like a deadly disease. It can start in a small way; spread quickly and have devastating effects, bringing weakness, restriction and sickness to the vibrant life of any individual. I'm sure everyone has at some time or other experienced discouragement. One of the ways that we can be strengthened against its effect, and better able to help others, is by recognising the various doors through which it comes.

These doors are:

Firstly – *Disappointment*
When our hopes have been dashed and our dreams shattered. Perhaps we've looked to somebody who has let us down; or maybe we find ourselves asking the question, 'Why did God allow that to happen?' It's then that discouragement comes in. What starts as disappointment can soon bring us to the place of being despondent, disillusioned and downcast. We see this with the two disciples who were walking along the Emmaus road. They had looked to Jesus as the answer to their struggles and hope

77

for their future, but then He was taken and crucified. As they walked down that road, their disappointment is expressed as they say,

> *'But we had hoped that he was the one to redeem Israel. Yes, and besides all this, it is now the third day since this happened.'* (Luke 24:21)

When we are unable to see the whole picture and things don't happen in the way we expect, the door of disappointment begins to open. Perhaps healing hasn't come when we've believed for it. An unconverted loved one or backslidden son or daughter appears unchanged, though we've prayed long and hard. We've asked for guidance but still the way ahead is uncertain. It's at times like these that disappointment creeps in and becomes like seeds of discouragement sown in our heart.

Secondly – *Frustration*

I heard a story recently of someone who wanted her friend to enrol in an aerobics class. 'Absolutely not!' exclaimed the friend in response to the invitation. 'I've already tried it once.' 'What happened?' asked the other person somewhat puzzled. 'Well,' she replied, 'I went and twisted, hopped, jumped, stretched and pulled and by the time I'd got that wretched leotard on, the class was over!'

Some experiences of frustration can be quite amusing but this is not always the case. Imagine how discouraged those fishermen must have felt when they came back cold, tired and wet, having fished all night and caught nothing (Luke 5:5). Their frustration must have left them feeling, 'What's the point?, it's a waste of time!' They'd fished in the same lake, used the same methods and worked hard, but there was nothing to show for it.

At times we can experience this same frustration in evangelism, church growth or in our particular areas of ministry. In spite of all our hard work, best efforts and doing the right things there are occasions when no visible results can be seen. In our working environment as well, if there's a feeling of frustration to reach certain targets or set goals we will feel discouraged.

This can also be the case in relationships too. One lady who came out for help at a meeting in Warminster, said that she felt a deep sense of frustration. Her father was a perfectionist and always looked for her to excel in everything. She tried to live up to his expectations and please him, but as hard as she tried it was never quite good enough. An added pressure was that her sister and brothers were good at most things. Because of all this she continually lived under a cloud of frustration.

Thirdly – *Loneliness*

Albert Einstein, the famous mathematician and physicist, once said, 'It's strange to be known so universally and yet to be so lonely.' God has made us for intimacy and companionship with others which is why His word says,

> *'It is not good for the man to be alone...'*
> (Genesis 2:18)

One definition of loneliness is, 'The lack of any deep, meaningful relationship with anyone'. This is why it is possible to feel lonely even in a crowded room; to laugh along with others but still feel empty inside. Loneliness has been termed the most desolate word in the English language. For many today it can be experienced not just as a single, divorced or widowed person, but where you would least expect it, within a marriage. You can live in the same house, eat at the same table, sleep in the same bed and raise children together, yet still feel desperately lonely inside. When a person is like this their life becomes open to discouragement and is the cause of so many falling into despair.

We learn an important lesson from the fall of Elijah regarding this. From being a man of 'Faith and Power', he became so discouraged that to die seemed his best option.

All his strength and victory was shattered, because of feeling alone at a time of crisis. He cried out,

> '... *I only, am left; and they seek my life, to take it away.*'
> (1 Kings 19:10b)

In reality there must have been many around cheering him on as he called upon God to send fire from heaven. There were other people nearby when the prophets of Baal were being slain. The fact was though, he had chosen to run away and isolate himself when he needed others the most. Discouragement and defeat need never have got the better of him if only his reaction had been more like the Apostles in the New Testament. When they were persecuted, beaten, imprisoned and threatened, they responded quite differently. We read of them that,

> '*When they were released they went to their friends...*'
> (Acts 4:23)

Then having done this, they got together and prayed for more boldness to face fearlessly the opposition!

Fourthly – *A Wounded Spirit*

The old saying, 'sticks and stones may break my bones but names will never hurt me,' is so untrue. Words can hurt and bring a great deal of discouragement into people's lives. What others say can either build our lives up and strengthen us or completely devastate and discourage us.

In Moses we find an example of this. The children of Israel considered him to be a wonderful leader whom they would follow anywhere. However, when they experienced hardship and trials they turned on Moses and Aaron and started to speak against them. In Numbers chapter 14 we find they all began to 'murmur' (verse 2). This developed into them saying, '*Let us choose a captain, and go back to Egypt*' (verse 4). Then eventually we read, '*All the congregation said to stone them with stones*' (verse 10). The pain and discouragement this brought to Moses must have been immense. He was doing his best. The problems weren't his fault and after all he didn't want the job in the first place! Their earlier grumblings had already caused him to say,

> *'I am not able to carry all this people alone, the burden is too heavy for me.'* (Numbers 11:14)

This must have now been the last straw.

When we are criticized, taken for granted, blamed for something unjustly or unkind things are said about us, discouragement knocks us flat. This is why the Bible says,

> *'A man's spirit sustains him in sickness, but a crushed spirit who can bear?'* (Proverbs 18:14, NIV)

For this reason we ought to be more careful about the things we say to others, especially about our leaders, and we need to take every opportunity to encourage them.

The Consequences of Discouragement

You don't need a lot of discernment to be able to identify someone who is struggling with discouragement. The effect it has upon a person's life is so powerful that the consequences are very difficult to hide. Even those who at times can smile, will not be able to conceal their feelings for long. Let us consider four of the areas where it becomes most obvious.

(a) Motivation

Joy and enthusiasm will begin to ebb away in the life of a discouraged person. They will feel empty and flat inside, like a glass of lukewarm Coca-Cola that has lost its fizz! Because, *'... the joy of the Lord is your strength'* (Nehemiah 8:10b), the effect will be that misery weakens your spiritual power. Once this happens, motivation begins to disappear so that it feels easier just to settle down and let things slide. A person's life then starts to dry up and their experience becomes like a wilderness where everything is barren and lifeless. This is why the Bible says,

> *'A cheerful heart is good medicine, but a downcast spirit dries up the bones.'* (Proverbs 17:22)

A Pentecostal minister from Birmingham asked for prayer after a meeting I'd spoken at. He'd been discouraged by hurtful, unjust comments that others, particularly another minister, had made about him. Rumours that were completely without foundation, had started circulating, and negative conclusions reached by those who had heard them. The effect upon this gifted, sincere man of God was quite devastating. It had knocked him so badly that he said he'd lost all his motivation and joy and felt as though he was just 'going through the motions'.

(b) Expectation

Discouragement has the effect of leaving people with a low level of expectancy. We should have great expectation because we have got a great God! However, when we've experienced a series of knocks, and we've tried our best but nothing seems to change, then we struggle. The great temptation is to take on board the mentality that God's blessing and promises are outside of our reach. We just don't expect to be able to lay hold of them like other people can.

Recently I heard a tale about a man who was driving along a country road, when he noticed a chicken that was keeping up with the speed of his car. He stepped on the accelerator and at 40 mph the chicken was still with him. The same was true at 50 mph and by the time he was doing 100 mph the chicken was out in front! As the chicken sped past him, he noticed that it had three legs. Suddenly as he watched, the bird made a sharp turn and the man followed it down a lane and into a farm yard. On meeting the farmer the driver said, 'I notice that all of your chickens

82

have three legs, did you develop the breed specially?' 'Yes,' the farmer replied, 'We all like drumsticks at home, so I came up with the idea of a three legged chicken!' 'How do they taste?' the man asked curiously. 'Blowed if I know,' replied the farmer, 'I haven't been able to catch one yet!'

This is what it's like if we're discouraged. We'll be able to see the excitement of other people's ideas and what seems amazing might be close to hand, but it'll always feel just outside of our grasp.

(c) Communication
The Bible says,

> '... Out of the abundance of the heart the mouth speaks.' (Matthew 12:34b)

When people are experiencing discouragement it will always, eventually, come out in the things they say. They will begin not only to feel despair but to communicate it as well. Comments that express defeatism, resentment, and anger will soon begin to slip out.

I remember counselling a man who was going through a very difficult period in his life. He'd recently come to know Christ as Saviour and made a genuine commitment to the Lord. Not long after his conversion though, he'd become unemployed and his situation remained unchanged for several years. On top of this problem there were considerable strains on his marriage. He prayed and believed God to provide work and to help in the difficulties of his relationship, but everything seemed to be crumbling around him. As I sat talking in his front room, trying to encourage him, he became very bitter and angry in his conversation. Pointing to the ceiling he stood up shouting in anger, 'God if you're there, I curse you to your face!' Obviously this man was at the end of himself and these were the words of someone struggling with extreme frustration. We too though, in perhaps less dramatic and serious ways, can find our speech just as offensive to God, when we get into such a place of discouragement.

(d) Resignation

Having been hurt by someone's actions or words, our discouragement often ends in resignation. Perhaps we've felt unappreciated, squashed or frustrated, maybe let down and disappointed, or conscious of failing in something. It's then we feel like 'throwing in the towel'. At times we lose heart because people oppose us. Sometimes we feel like giving in because we are physically and emotionally exhausted. For whatever reason, we grow tired and are tempted to give up. God's word will always urge us to keep going and not resign. It says,

> *'Let us not grow weary in well-doing, for in due season we shall reap, if we do not lose heart.'* (Galatians 6:9)

I read of a minister who felt so discouraged and defeated that he was ready to give in to his circumstances. One morning as he sat dejectedly by the window, he looked outside and noticed a starling perched on the sill. The bird seemed to look steadily at him and chirp what sounded like, 'Give it up!, Give it up!' The pastor thought about his frustration and discouragement, wondering if this was perhaps God's word to him. At that moment the pastor's wife came into the room, she too listened and then laughed. Turning to her husband she said with a smile, 'Why, that starling is not saying, "Give it up!, Give it up!" but "Keep it up!"'

The Cure for Discouragement

Because discouragement is like a 'deadly disease' which eats away at people, it is vital that steps are taken to do something about the problem. The principles that lead to recovery need to be applied without delay, in just the same way as if we had a physical ailment and received a prescription from the doctor. Following carefully his counsel and applying the appropriate medicine would enable us to begin to rise from our sickbed.

Firstly

Begin by opening up to someone about the way we feel. This is especially important for men who try so hard to hide their feelings, but of course it is important for everyone. Rather than suppressing discouragement and sweeping the matter under the carpet, there must be reality about our true condition. David realizing this says,

> 'Behold, thou desirest truth in the inward being...'
>
> (Psalm 51:6)

We need to bring our feelings out into the light. Always remember that the devil works in the darkness and God works in the light! All the while we try to hide or pretend, the enemy has a stronghold in our life. The moment we bring the matter into the light by sharing with someone, there comes a release of that oppression. Just to be able to talk with another person about what we're going through, and to have someone share the burden, seems to bring a lightness to our spirit.

In our willingness to be honest about our feelings, we'll probably find that we've had wrong attitudes towards someone because of what we've experienced. This may also include resentment towards God which needs to be dealt with.

A lady from Stoke came for counsel and prayer after a meeting. She shared about her resentment towards God because He had not provided her with a husband. She was discouraged because for years this was her priority in prayer and she felt God had let her down. Her words to me were, 'If only the Lord would give me a husband, then **everything** would be alright in my life!' I tried to share about the need to repent of her attitude towards God. Also to change her priorities and put Jesus first in her life, rather than the desire for a husband. Unfortunately though, she became so angry and resentful towards me, that she just stormed out of the room!

Secondly

In all our frustration and disappointment we need to make a commitment before God not to give up. We must choose to go on believing His word and re-affirm our faith that God will honour His promise which says,

> *'Take delight in the Lord, and he will give you the desires of your heart.'* (Psalm 37:4)

God will always honour those who in their faith honour Him. His promise may not come as quickly as we'd like and so the Bible therefore encourages to be,

> *'imitators of those who through faith and patience inherit the promises.'* (Hebrews 6:12)

There is a marvellous poem written by an unknown author that has always been such a help and encouragement to me on this point. It's words are:

> 'When things go wrong as they sometimes will,
> When the road you're trudging seems all uphill,
> When the funds are low and the debts are high
> And you want to smile but you have to sigh,
> When care is pressing you down a bit,
> Rest, if you must, but don't you quit.
> Life is queer with its twists and turns,
> As every one of us sometimes learns,
> And many a failure turns about
> When he might have won had he stuck it out.
> Don't give up though the pace seems slow –
> You may succeed with another blow.
> Success is failure turned inside out
> The silver tint of the cloud of doubt.

And you never can tell how close you are –
It may be near when it seems so far.
So stick to the fight when you're hardest hit:
It's when things seem worst you must not quit.'

Someone who had an attitude of commitment never to give in was the Apostle Paul. In spite of all his struggles and hardship he refused to allow his circumstances to get on top of him. This is why he could say,

> 'We are afflicted in every way, but not crushed; perplexed, but not driven to despair; persecuted, but not forsaken; struck down, but not destroyed.'
>
> (2 Corinthians 4:8 & 9)

Thirdly

Realise that where mistakes have been made, it's not the end of the world! We're not perfect, and as long as we learn from them, the very thing that we're getting despondent about need not have the final word in our lives.

A story that illustrates how prone we are to making mistakes comes from an incident that happened at Harrod's some years ago. During a busy morning at the cheese counter, a new assistant had been left to deal with telephone enquiries. Suddenly there was a call that caused all the colour to drain from the young womans face. 'Please hold on,' she whispered nervously to the caller, 'I'll fetch the buyer.' Quickly finding him she anxiously said, 'It's Buckingham Palace and they want 18 lbs of Cheddar!' The buyer excused himself from a queue of customers and went briskly to his office to speak to the caller. A few minutes later he reappeared, 'You did the right thing,' he assured the newcomer, 'but so that you know in future, the Prince of Wales is a pub on the other side of the Brompton Road!'

The person who has never made any mistakes has never done anything! The Bible is full of those who made major errors. Moses acted in the flesh and killed an Egyptian.

Abraham grew impatient and rather than waiting for God's promise of a child to be fulfilled through Sarah, he took a slave girl to have that child. David committed adultery with Bathsheba and then manipulated the death of the woman's husband. Samson also fell to the lust of immorality. Jonah ran away from God's commission to go to Nineveh. Peter denied Christ. Mark deserted the apostolic mission and Paul at one time, though religious, was a murderer, persecutor of Christians and blasphemer of the faith.

The wonderful thing that we must always remind ourselves of, is that God will never cast us away because of our shortcomings. If we sin or make mistakes, but are willing to learn from them, then He will always bring us through to fulfil His purpose. The Bible says,

> 'I am sure that he who began a good work in you will bring it to completion at the day of Christ.'
>
> (Philippians 1:6)

Fourthly

Don't just lie down and accept discouraging circumstances. We need to take action to do something about them. No matter how great the odds might be against us, God is able to find a way where there seems to be no way. Even in those situations that appear impossible the Bible says,

> 'With men this is impossible, but with God all things are possible.' (Matthew 19:26b)

We must use our imagination and be creative, so that we don't just resign ourselves to the inevitable.

One person who employed his imagination in solving a Goliath-size problem was a small shopkeeper. When developers built a gleaming bright supermarket and gigantic discount house on either side of his tiny general store he took action. Undaunted, he scraped together his savings

88

and purchased an eye catching, bright Neon sign. When he placed this right over the front of his store, between the two giant competitors, it read, 'MAIN ENTRANCE HERE!'

Fifthly

Let God's word and not man's be the final authority in your life. He sees not just what we are at the moment but what we will become. This was very much the case in Gideon's life as he was nervously hiding from the Midianites, threshing out corn in a wine press. The word of the Lord came to him saying, *'you mighty man of valour'* (Judges 6:12b). God wasn't being sarcastic but He could see in Gideon great potential, even though it wasn't apparent to anyone else.

We should be encouraged by the ability that God has placed within each of us. He sees our potential and we must not be too concerned with the opinions of other people. More often than not, because their estimation of us is only viewed on a superficial level, they can be completely wrong. For example, Beethoven's music teacher said of him, when he was young, 'As a composer he was hopeless!' When W.F. Woolworth was 21 he got a job in a store but was not allowed to serve customers because it was said, 'He didn't have enough sense!' Walt Disney was once fired by a newspaper editor because it was thought, 'He had no good ideas!' Caruso the world famous singer was told by one teacher when he was a boy that, 'He couldn't sing and had no voice at all!' We must never let other people's opinions, our own self doubts or the devil's lies minimise the tremendous potential within us.

The judgement of man concerning our ability is so often formed from a great deal of prejudice and narrow mindedness. It is those who refuse to listen to the unscriptural views of others, who will go on to fulfil their destiny. The French laughed at Napoleon's youth when he sought to obtain a seat in the Chamber of Deputies; he replied, 'Men mature quickly on the battlefield, and gentlemen it is from the battlefield that I have come.' Needless to say he won his seat!

To overcome discouragement we need to submit our thoughts and emotions to the authority of God's word, even when it doesn't make sense. The disciples that had been so discouraged by their inability to catch fish on that all night fishing trip followed this principle. Because they did, they were tremendously encouraged by the outcome. Jesus said,

> 'Put out into the deep and let down your nets for a catch,' and Peter replied, 'Master, we toiled all night and took nothing! But **at your word** I will let down the nets.'
> (Luke 5:4 &5)

It was as they brought their feelings and thinking into subjection to God's word that they were encouraged by a net breaking, boat sinking load! (Luke 5:6 & 7).

Sixthly

Don't take life too seriously. We need to lighten up and not receive everything as a personal attack against ourselves. Sometimes we can misinterpret the comments of others. Their remarks may not always have been intended in the way we received them. We should be a bit more generous and give people the benefit of the doubt. Even remarks made that were perhaps insensitive, need not have a discouraging effect upon us, if we try to see the funny side of them.

I was amused by a newspaper article about a Norfolk vicar who told an elderly parishioner that he would soon be retiring and would be very sorry to leave the area. 'But,' he said, trying to reassure her, 'Never mind, you'll probably get a better man when I go.' 'Not necessarily,' she replied comfortingly, 'That's what the last parson said before he left!'

If we can learn not to be quite so sensitive but a little more long-suffering with people we'll find that it will save us an awful lot of discouragement. The only way this is possible is when we are truly willing to die to ourselves, and be filled with the love of Christ for others. We then begin to see the practical out-working of God's word that says,

> *'Love bears all things, believes all things, hopes all things, endures all things.'*   (1 Corinthians 13:7)

Seventhly

Find at least one thing that you can give thanks to God for and dwell on that. This I believe is one of the most helpful and practical principles in enabling us to rise up from discouragement. I firmly believe it is possible to do this in any situation that could otherwise potentially devastate or discourage us. No matter how grave and awful it might appear, there will always be one thing we can be grateful about. If, rather than dwelling on the gloom, hurt and injustice of whatever might have happened, we start to look for that one thing to rejoice in, then our attitude will begin to change. This is why the Bible says,

> *'give thanks in all circumstances; for this is the will of God in Christ Jesus for you.'*   (1 Thessalonians 5:18)

There are some things which are so difficult and unrighteous that we can't thank God 'for' them. However, 'in' everything we can still have a grateful heart that acknowledges God's faithfulness and ultimate sovereignty.

The prophet Habakkuk shows us an excellent example of this principle. He was surrounded by extremely hard circumstances. There was so much to discourage him, if he'd allowed it to. However, he was determined that 'in' his situation he was going to be grateful to God. We read,

> *'Though the fig tree do not blossom, nor fruit be on the vines, the produce of the olive fail, and the fields yield*

91

no food, the flock be cut off from the fold and there be no herd in the stalls, yet I will rejoice in the Lord, I will joy in the God of my salvation.'

(Habakkuk 3:17 & 18)

Chapter 6

Overcoming Insecurity

Many subtle lies, aimed at influencing our thinking, are fed to us today from the advertising world, particularly via the medium of television. Through cleverly presented adverts we're told such things as, 'Happiness is a cigar called Hamlet!' – 'For the perfect complexion, simply wash with Camay soap!' – 'To be irresistibly attractive to men, use just a touch of Impulse perfume!'

One of the most ridiculous adverts that appeared on our screens not so long ago, brought the enthusiastic message that, 'Brushing your teeth with Colgate toothpaste will transform your personality, giving you a bright ring of confidence!' – if only life was that simple! For people to know real confidence, they need far more than Colgate paste in their mouths. Only divine conviction and God's power in their hearts will ever make any difference. We have a false sense of security and deceive ourselves, if our trust is in anything but the Lord.

Among the most common problems that I find today, is a deep sense of insecurity in so many people. Feelings of inadequacy and inferiority seem to dominate their lives robbing them of confidence to live life to the full. Frequently I've had people come to me saying that they long to be able to pray publicly in a meeting, but are too self-conscious. Others desire to witness more effectively but are afraid. Some want to move out in the gifts of the Holy Spirit, know a greater freedom in praise and worship or simply have more confidence at work and in relationships, but they just feel held back. In all of these areas of difficulty it is insecurity that restricts their development.

Characteristics of an Insecure Person

Someone who has little or no confidence at all and is controlled by feelings of insecurity will have specific characteristics in their life that stand out clearly.

(1) They will be nervously anxious about what people think or might be saying about them behind their backs. Always looking for the approval and acceptance of others, they will often be indecisive. This is because of the fear of doing or saying the wrong thing and losing favour with those around them. Insecurity causes them to feel that they must be constantly proving themselves to others. The result of this will be a continual striving and inability to relax and be themselves.

(2) Some insecure people are very 'prickly' and extremely difficult to get on with. They will be over-sensitive and defensive, taking everything that is said personally and any criticism as a direct attack against them. They will often be trying to justify what they say and do, particularly when things go wrong. As a consequence, they will build an invisible wall of self-protection around themselves to keep people at a safe distance. These people will have few, if any deep friendships. Their suspicion of other people's motives, and their inability to sustain relationships, will cause them to be very lonely people.

(3) Because of feelings of inferiority and inadequacy, insecure people especially find 'eyeball contact' with others something they avoid. Their deep sense of worthlessness and the way they under-estimate their ability results in self-consciousness and low self-esteem dominating their life. Memories sharp with the details of past failures, cause them to express negative comments like, 'I'm

no good,' 'I'm always making a mess of things,' 'Nothing ever goes right for me,' 'Other people could do the job much better than I could,' etc. Due to feelings of low self-worth they will normally be introvert in their personality and find it very difficult to give and receive love. Expressing their emotions in any open, natural way will be extremely hard because they feel unworthy of being loved.

(4) In contrast, for some who struggle with insecurity, there will be a lot of unreality and escapism into a fantasy world of their own. Living behind a mask of pretence they can appear to be outwardly confident. This might be expressed by being over-talkative, or through loud attention-seeking behaviour, to the extreme of being domineering and manipulative. They may look secure and competent, and can even appear to be the 'life and soul of the party', but in reality they are desperately trying to hide their feelings of inadequacy. Such people are afraid to open up and share how they feel. Their fear is that when people discover what they are really like they will be rejected, so they live in this world of deception.

(5) Another characteristic of the insecure person is always feeling threatened by the challenge to do something that they've never done before. They will settle to live life in mediocrity, never becoming what they have the potential to be in their personal life, at work, or in the Church. The challenge to develop and grasp new opportunities as they arise is something they'd rather let pass by. Change is also very intimidating to them and they would much rather stay in the same place, doing the same thing, in the same way they've always done it. For them there is safety in the 'known' and what they have become used to.

The Causes of Insecurity

When a baby is born into the world it has an immense amount of needs. Everyone has four basic needs that must be met continually throughout life if they are to feel secure and whole. These are:

- the *need to be loved,*
- the *need to belong,*
- the *need to be considered a person of worth* and
- the *need for a sense of purpose and achievement.*

Unless these areas are met, people become damaged emotionally, scarred in their personality and hindered in discovering their full ability.

There is not a question of doubt in my mind, that countless thousands of Christians are currently battling with present day problems, because of past events. People can be wounded and damaged inside, in a way that no one else knows about, except in how it manifests itself through the characteristics we've mentioned. Their perception of themselves, others and even God is distorted by what they have experienced over many years, right from childhood. Some of the reasons for such problems are:

(a) Parental Rejection and Lack of Love

One of the major causes of insecurity comes from being raised in an unhappy home. Perhaps in circumstances where the parents were divorced, or maybe stayed together but created an atmosphere of tension and hostility.

Also, having parents who are simply too busy to give sufficient attention and time to their child, will sow seeds of insecurity. An article in the *Sunday Correspondent* bears out this point. It said,

> 'Thousands of children are suffering from stress because their parents are just to busy to talk to them. On average parents spend as little as two minutes a day really talking to their children. A survey of 4,000 American Primary School pupils found nearly half showed alarming levels of insecurity and stressful behaviour. This included, temper tantrums, sleeplessness, stomach pains and constant headaches. Parents would talk to them on average, for around 14 minutes a day – but 12 of those minutes would be spent discussing what food there was to eat.'

Living in a home where little or no affection is seen between mum and dad, or expressed from them to the child, also dramatically affects the security of that individual. A deacon I met after a preaching engagement at Gravesend in Kent, could identify with this. He approached me for help in response to the subject I'd spoken on, regarding the 'Fatherhood of God'. He said, 'I can't relate to God as my father like you've spoken about tonight because we had a father in our home who ruled by fear!'

A deep effect upon a child's confidence results when few positive words of encouragement are spoken. The simple affirmation of the child's ability in terms like, 'Well done' or, 'That's really good,' needs to be expressed. In some homes rather than this positive affirmation being heard, negative 'name tags' are given which can be like a curse on the child's life. Thoughtless, insensitive and unkind words like, 'You're useless,' 'You'll never amount to anything very much,' 'You're stupid, clumsy, ugly,' etc. The cruel reference to the child being an 'accident' and not really wanted or the parents preferring a girl to a boy, can also be very destructive and bring a great deal of insecurity.

Someone once said,

'The beginning of our life is like the bud of a flower. It must receive the warmth of human love and assurance, and the nourishment of parental affection if it is to open and expose the unique beauty God has placed within each individual. If the bud is injured by hostile forces like an unseasonable frost it will not open. So too is a person who is without the warmth and encouragement of love, and who must endure the chilling absence of praise and affection, they will remain closed in on themselves.'

(b) Traumatic Events Deeply Embedded in the Emotions

A whole range of experiences like sexual, emotional or

physical abuse can destroy a person's confidence and shatter their self-esteem. I remember one occasion, taking a meeting at St Ives in Cornwall, when a Christian lady came forward for prayer. She shared about her feelings of insecurity and fear, particularly towards men. As she spoke of her inability to trust anyone, I could sense the emotional defensive wall which she had built around herself. In talking together she told me that at the age of four years she was raped by a man who was taking her to Sunday School! Her whole life was devastated, and from that point something died within that little girl. Although she grew physically into adulthood, emotionally she was still like a child and 40 years later still suffered the consequences of that tragedy.

As well as the awful trauma of rape and abuse, which is becoming more and more common today, other events can have a big impact upon a person. For example, the shock of being involved in a serious road accident; having your house broken into by burglars; perhaps being attacked when very young by a large dog; or the sudden death of someone very close, who at the time provided great security and dependence.

Through traumatic events the measure of confidence which may once have been there can be lost. While ministering at a church in Stoke-on-Trent I noticed the absence of a Christian lady who was normally always at the meeting. Having asked after her, I was told that several months ago she was mugged and her handbag was stolen. The shock of this brought such great fear into her life, that all her confidence to go out had gone, and she had confined herself to the security and safety of her home.

(c) Unfavourable Comparisons

The way we feel inside about ourselves is very important. When we consciously or subconsciously consider that we're not as good as those around us, either in performance or as people, we then find ourselves with underlying feelings of insecurity.

This situation is not helped at all when others make unfavourable comparisons between ourselves and someone else. Particularly when it starts within the family as we're growing up and then is reinforced at school by teachers. Comments like, 'Why can't you be like your sister, she doesn't make those sort of mistakes' or, 'You're nothing like your brother, he picks things up so much more quickly than you.' These comparisons can be very damaging to those concerned.

I'll never forget an elderly lady some years ago, who came seeking help. She was a Christian, but had been greatly damaged emotionally by the names and comments people had made about her throughout her life. From childhood she was continually put down by her parents and school friends. This left her with no confidence at all. She shared with me that often when entering her own church, she would go into the cloakroom and cling tightly on to the coats of the people who were in the meeting. She desperately wanted to be loved and to give love, but because of feeling worthless, she believed nobody would ever want to love her.

There can also be unfavourable comparisons that we make ourselves, as was mentioned in a previous chapter on 'Anxiety'. Looking at our peers or the role models we see in glossy magazines we become dissatisfied with who we are and so try to imitate others. Preoccupied by their beauty, talent, intellect and personality and constantly wishing we were more like them, we undermine our own value as unique individuals. There is so much pressure put upon people today from the world of modelling, fashion and films etc. If we haven't the 'perfect' figure, the 'right' looks, or the same ability, then we feel we are not normal and there is something wrong with us.

(d) A Series of Knocks and Set-backs

Most people would expect to have the occasional set-back or problem in their lives. Some though, certainly seem to have more than their share of difficulties. For example, experiences of pressure at work which are then carried over into the home, where conflict and tension brings its strain upon relationships. The inevitable occasions of frustration and disappointment in the church. Plans that don't materialise, or prayers that seem to go unanswered. When we have a series of these knocks, and it seems as though it's just one thing on top of another, then not only are we discouraged but our faith can be shaken. This might cause us to lose confidence in our own worth and in the fact that God is for us.

A New Creation in Christ

While preaching at a church in Manchester several years ago, a Pastor came to me after the meeting, to express his disagreement with something I'd said. It was about the influence of past experiences affecting our present day lives as Christians. The basis for his argument was the scripture,

> 'If any one is in Christ, he is a new creation; the old has passed away, behold, the new has come.'
>
> (2 Corinthians 5:17)

His assertion was that because the work of the cross was complete, then when we become Christians our past lives no longer have any bearing on how we live. Therefore, we should have no present day problems coming from previous damaging experiences.

This is certainly not an untypical view in the Church today. However, I believe it does great harm to those that have been shaken badly by very real traumas, and the cruel actions and attitudes of others towards them. The result of such naivety causes people to feel guilty about the fact that they still have problems. It forces them to live in pretence, denying that they have unresolved issues from the past for fear of the disapproval of more 'spiritual' Christians. Ultimately what happens is that it compounds their problem, leaving them feeling failures, condemned and isolated.

The well known Bible teacher and author Selwyn Hughes, speaking about this says;

> 'Conversion is not a magic "cure all" where we go to bed one night, hand God our difficult personality and hurtful past, then when we wake up the next morning we find that our life has changed completely and our past no longer a problem.'

The same point is also made by that excellent preacher Dr Martyn Lloyd-Jones. When talking about our conversion he says,

> 'The fundamental elements in our personality and temperament are not changed by conversion and re-birth. The new man means a new disposition, a new understanding and a new orientation, but the man himself psychologically is essentially the same.'

Some Church leaders are understandably cautious about this, because there are many dubious streams of counselling around today, particularly in the area of 'Inner Healing' and 'Healing of the Memories'. Such teaching can present counselling methods that rely more on psychology than the power of Christ, and are not only without scriptural basis, but in some cases are contrary to God's word. Those who are always digging and delving around with the past and focusing on the problem, instead of believing in the truth of God's word to bring release, can do more harm than good.

There is also the undeniable fact that endless numbers of people come with problems, who enjoy the attention, love and time given to them by counsellors prepared to listen to their difficulties. This can produce 'perpetual counsellees', people who will always be wanting help on the same issues relating to their past. They never seem to be moving on, because deep down they don't want to face up to the responsibility of walking in freedom.

While these things are true, we must never swing away to the other extreme of saying to damaged people, 'All you have to do is have more faith, just look to the cross and believe in the finished work of Jesus!' I accept that Christ's work on the cross is complete and there is nothing that we can possibly add to it. Everything that needs to be done for our release and victory has already been accomplished. However, the 'New Creation' we become through our initial repentance and commitment to Christ is only the start of that process of change. We have to acknowledge our 'hang-ups' and problems, as the Holy Spirit reveals them. Then by faith bring them to that finished work, to appropriate what has already been provided for us.

It seems a paradox – the miracle of being a *'new creation in Christ'*, and yet still being affected by problems from the past. The reality is though, **The *new* will never fully come into our lives until the *old* has fully passed away**. In some cases we hold on to the old and in others, the old holds on to us, either way, it's still true. Throughout our Christian walk, our lives are in a process of being changed. This is why the Bible says,

> *'And we all, with unveiled face, beholding the glory of the Lord, are being changed into his likeness from one degree of glory to another . . . '* (2 Corinthians 3:18)

It's only as we grow in faith, believing in all that Christ has accomplished, that this new nature becomes more evident in our lives.

If we simply try to suppress and bury the problems of our past (which is how many deal with their painful experiences), we will bury them alive and not dead! They will continue to have an inhibiting influence upon us. Only by bringing these areas to the cross are we able to see the

102

power of them broken. It is then by faith in God's word that we can say,

> *'I have been crucified with Christ; it is no longer I who live, but Christ who lives in me; and the life I now live in the flesh I live by faith in the Son of God, who loved me and gave himself for me.'*　　　　　(Galatians 2:20)

How to Develop Confidence

For a solid foundation to be laid, upon which confidence and security can be built, it is necessary first of all to clear the ground. We need to make sure all the 'rubbish' that is getting in the way and hindering our development is removed. To do this we must **firstly** – *confess* any area of unbelief in God's word and God's power. **Secondly** – *renounce* the lies that we have been believing and the negative way we've felt about ourselves. Then **thirdly** – *seek*, where appropriate, deliverance from any area of demonic oppression like, the spirit of fear, rejection, insecurity, torment etc. Also, where there is a wounded spirit at the root of the problem we need to look to God who alone is able to heal our emotions; not through any psychological techniques or constant looking back to the past, but by faith in His word which says;

> *'The Lord is near to the brokenhearted, and saves the crushed in spirit.'*　　　　　(Psalm 34:18)

And again in Psalm 147:3,

> *'He heals the brokenhearted, and binds up their wounds.'*

Having come to this point we are now able to begin to build upon this firm foundation with God's word of truth. Our aim is to see the greatness of **His** love towards us and develop a positive understanding of the strength He can bring to our lives. Faith in our relationship with God is the only way that confidence and security begin to grow. When we have confidence before God then it will influence every other area of our living.

In Psalm 27 we find someone who had a tremendous confidence in the Lord and we see the impact it had upon his life. From this we can discover some clear principles that enable us to progress to a place of security. These words were the expression of a man who knew, not just theoretically, but from personal experience, what confidence was all about. David had wrestled and defeated a bear. He had tackled and killed a lion. This is the man who stood against the terror of Goliath and defeated him with just a sling. He was the person who was mighty in battle against God's enemies and of whom all of Israel's women sang,

> *'Saul has slain his thousands, and David his ten thousands.'* (1 Samuel 18:7b)

Let us consider then these characteristics regarding his confidence.

(1) He had an unshakeable faith that God alone was the security of his life. David could say,

> *'The Lord is my light and my salvation; whom shall I fear? The Lord is the stronghold of my life; of whom shall I be afraid.'* (Psalm 27:1)

Our confidence comes not from our own ability, position, success or possessions, but completely from our personal relationship of faith in God. As the Bible says,

> *'Let not the wise man glory in his wisdom, let not the mighty man glory in his might, let not the rich man glory in his riches; but let him who glories glory in this, that he understands and knows me . . .'*
> (Jeremiah 9:23 & 24)

(2) David had an attitude of heart and mind that refused to allow negative fear to affect him,

> *'Though a host encamp against me, my heart shall not fear; though war arise against me, yet I will be confident.'*
> (Psalm 27:3)

The challenges that confront us, which we'd rather avoid, or run away from, we must stand up to and be prepared to take them on. In all that would try to make us fearful, we need to assert our will, release our faith, and choose to be victors and not victims!

(3) David had a passionate desire to make sure that his first and all important priority was to be in God's presence.

> *'One thing I have asked of the Lord, that will I seek after; that I may dwell in the house of the Lord all the days of my life, to behold the beauty of the Lord, and to enquire in his temple.'*
> (Psalm 27:4)

In this day and age of materialism, the temptation is to be entangled in the pursuit of so many meaningless and shallow things. We need to be constantly on our guard that we are walking in the Spirit, knowing the presence of God in all that we do. This will require a discipline to make sure that nothing distracts our appreciation of the beauty and preciousness of the Lord.

(4) David had an absolute assurance that God was watching over his life, not only to protect but to bring victory. Convinced that God was for him, he knew that the Lord would respond to each crisis as it presented itself.

> *'For he will hide me in his shelter in the day of trouble; he will conceal me under the cover of his tent, he will set me high upon a rock.'*
> (Psalm 27:5)

We must be realistic about the trials and troubles of life. They will come, nobody is immune from them, but when they confront us, we can be assured that, *'The battle is the Lord's.'*

(5) David had a praising heart even when faced with difficulties and understood that there was power and victory in praise.

> *'And now my head shall be lifted up above my enemies round about me; and I will offer in his tent sacrifices with shouts of joy; I will sing and make melody to the Lord.'* (Psalm 27:6)

The genuine shout of praise when faced with the enemies of our soul is the true expression of our confidence. If our hearts are full of faith then our mouths will be full of praise!

(6) David had a sensitivity to God's voice and an obedient heart towards God's instructions. He knew that in seeking after the Lord he would always find Him. Because he had learnt this basic principle his response was without hesitation,

> *'Thou has said, "Seek ye my face." My heart says to thee, "Thy face, Lord, do I seek."'* (Psalm 27:8)

When we feel threatened in any way and insecurity tries to creep in, our strength comes from listening for God's word and responding in instant obedience to what He says.

(7) David had a strong conviction that the blessings of God were for him now and not just in some future day.

> *'I believe that I shall see the goodness of the Lord in the land of the living!'* (Psalm 27:13)

The scriptures say,

> *'All the promises of God find their Yes in him.'*
> (2 Corinthians 1:20)

It is faith that enables us to move beyond a head knowledge of God's goodness, to a heart experience. Especially at those times when the memories of our past come before our mind and the temptation to turn inward, dwelling on our problems is there, we must choose to live by faith. As the Bible says,

> *'O taste and see that the Lord is good...'* (Psalm 34:8)

(8)   David knew the importance of waiting on God, of coming aside in the busyness of life and not rushing on ahead doing things in his own strength.

> *'Wait for the Lord; be strong, and let your heart take courage; yea, wait for the Lord.'*   (Psalm 27:14)

It is in that stillness before God we can hear the reassurance of His voice. As we discipline ourselves to wait for the Lord we receive that strength we need and we find ourselves receiving the courage to overcome whatever would try to make us afraid.

Perhaps in looking at the depth and quality of relationship that David had, we're tempted to feel we fall far short. This sense of failure in itself can tend to shake our confidence and affect our security, making us feel hopeless and inadequate. However, let us always remember that it was David who failed so greatly when committing adultery with Bathsheba, but because he was repentant God gave him a second chance. The Lord does not look for immediate perfection in any of us, but for a genuine desire to arrive at that place, and a humble spirit to acknowledge God as the only source of our security.

Chapter 7

Finding Guidance in Uncertainty

In 1939 while making his Christmas address to the people of this nation, King George VI spoke of his faith in God's guidance. World War II had begun, and Great Britain faced the onslaught of Hitler's reckless military barrage. As the King spoke on that Christmas Day, he concluded his remarks with these words written some thirty years earlier, by Minnie Louise Haskins:

> 'And I said to the man who stood at the gate of the year: "Give me a light that I may tread safely into the unknown." And he replied: "Go out into the darkness and put your hand into the hand of God. That shall be to you better than light and safer than a known way."'

Knowing God's guidance brings to us a tremendous sense of security, especially in times of uncertainty. Here is where we come to another major problem area. Many people today are confused about God's will for their lives. They are unclear about His purpose for themselves generally, and in particular when specific decisions need to be made.

The Importance of Knowing God's Will

Finding the will of God and remaining in it, is one of the most important priorities for us to have, because it touches every area of our lives. For example: what career we are to follow; whom we should marry; where we are to live; what our ministry and function is in the Church; when and how we are to move out in faith etc. Being sure about such things is important because, **Decision Determines Destiny!** If we are to get where God wants us to be and accomplish His will, then the fog of confusion and uncertainty must be dispelled. The choices that we make every single day affect not only the quality of our living, and fruitfulness of our service, but also our very destiny and at times even that of our families. We need to not merely make choices, but also to make the right ones if we are to know the blessing of walking in God's will. That which does not begin with God will ultimately end in failure. As the scripture says,

> *'Many are the plans in the mind of a man, but it is the purpose of the Lord that will be established.'*
>
> (Proverbs 19:21)

Wrong decisions can cause the great potential within us to be wasted. This is illustrated by the amazing but true story of a teenage girl in France. In the year 1403, one of the wealthiest men in Paris died, leaving his entire estate to his daughter. She was a beautiful young woman, and many men wanted to marry her, but she decided to give up her fortune and become a recluse. To isolate herself from society, she asked to be sealed into a cell within the wall of a church. The entrance was plastered shut, except for one small hole through which food could be passed. She was confined in that small area at the age of 18 years and remained there until she died at age 98. As I read about this, I couldn't help but think, what a tragically wasted life! Because of one misguided decision this woman had robbed God, others and herself of so much good that could have been accomplished.

The apostle Paul was a man who not only had a definite sense of God's direction for his own life, but also a great burden that others might be equally clear. He expressed this priority concern as he wrote to the Colossian Church,

> '... we have not ceased to pray for you, asking that you may be filled with the knowledge of his will in all spiritual wisdom and understanding, to lead a life worthy of the Lord, fully pleasing to him, bearing fruit in every good work and increasing in the knowledge of God.'
>
> (Colossians 1:9–10)

Paul expected every believer to be *'filled'* with the knowledge of God's will. In these verses we find four reasons why knowing the Lord's guidance is so vital for us all.

(a) That Our Lives Might be Worthy of the Lord
This indeed is a high calling and yet one each Christian is instructed in God's word to aim for. Paul says,

> 'Only let your manner of life be worthy of the gospel of Christ ... '
>
> (Philippians 1:27)

How we live before an ungodly and unbelieving world is very important. We can be sure that people are watching us carefully, to see if what we do matches up with what we say. It is quite a challenge to consider the question, 'If we were accused of being a Christian, would there be enough evidence to convict us?'

(b) That We Might be Fully Pleasing to God
The normal Christian life is seen in a consistent righteousness before the Lord. Not to be occasionally doing something acceptable to Him, or be partially living in obedience to His word, but that at any given moment God might be able to declare about us, as He did Jesus,

111

'This is my beloved Son, with whom I am well pleased.'
(Matthew 3:17b).

(c) That We Might be Fruitful in all our Work

When we are abiding in God's will in the same way a branch abides in the vine, we then find that in everything we do there will be fruitfulness. As God's word says,

'I am the vine, you are the branches. He who abides in me, and I in him, he it is that bears much fruit . . . '
(John 15:5)

(d) That We Might be Growing in the Knowledge of God

This of course is not merely a head knowledge but a heart experience. Walking in God's will, being led by His guidance, produces spiritual development and a knowledge of God that results in effective service. Our lives then begin to make an impact on others. This is why Paul's all consuming desire was expressed in the words,

'that I might know him and the power of His resurrection . . . '
(Philippians 3:10)

God Still Speaks Today

While reading through one of the national newspapers recently my attention was drawn to an unusual headline. In bold black letters were the words, 'THE SILENT CD'. Curiosity got the better of me, so I read on and this is what it said;

'Music lovers are snapping up a new compact disc, even though it is totally silent. Not a note is played on the so called piano recital, but hundreds of people have already paid £5.29 to purchase the disc! The chairman of the Noise Abatement Society has commented that, the silent CD is a welcome innovation!'

112

To think that people are actually paying money and listening to absolutely nothing is absurd, almost beyond belief. All I can say is, praise God as Christians we don't have to live pretending to hear God's voice. Nor need we sit around trying to imagine God speaking to us. The marvellous fact is, that in the uncertainty and confusion of life today, we can know God's voice directing us in all that we do. This is what the prophet Isaiah meant when he wrote,

> 'And your ears shall hear a word behind you, saying, "This is the way, walk in it," when you turn to the right or when you turn to the left.' (Isaiah 30:21)

In Psalm 29 there is one phrase that stands out prominently. Seven times, from verse 3–9, we read the words, 'The voice of the Lord.' What we need today more than anything else in the world is to hear God speak. One word from Him is worth more than ten thousand sermons and more valuable than all our debates, discussions and committee meetings. When God speaks just one word to us, it's like turning on a light in a dark room. Everything looks different, we begin to see clearly and all the vagueness is cast out!

God wants us to hear Him speak for He says,

> 'Call to me and I will answer you, and will tell you great and hidden things which you have not known.' (Jeremiah 33:3)

When we are uncertain about life's choices and the fog of confusion seems to surround us the Bible says,

> 'If any of you lacks wisdom, let him ask God, who gives to all men generously, ... But let him ask in faith, with no doubting...' (James 1:5–6)

The important thing is that each one of us must expect to hear His voice. We need to believe that He wants to speak to every individual. Not just the 'big names' or 'anointed preachers' of this world, but to us all. This is why Jesus said,

> *'He who belongs to God hears what God says.'*
>
> (John 8:47, NIV)

Recognising the Sound of God's Voice

An example of someone who didn't recognise the sound of God's voice is Samuel. He had the call of God upon his life and was raised in the temple being trained by Eli. When God began to speak to him though, he couldn't distinguish between the voice of man and the voice of the Lord (1 Samuel 3:4–10). God woke him three times from his sleep, calling him, but he assumed it was Eli speaking. Eventually, on the fourth occasion, it dawned on him that it was the Lord trying to get his attention, but there was no immediate recognition as to whose voice it was. Sometimes we can find ourselves in the same position and be missing the guidance God wants to bring, simply because we've not learnt to recognise His voice.

It's absolutely vital to discern what voice we are listening to, because there are many all around us, attempting to influence and direct our lives. There is the voice of an unbelieving world insisting, 'You can't believe what you can't see!' From the humanist, the indifferent and even the liberal Church there comes a stream of negative messages trying to shape our beliefs, and distort our thinking. In addition to these there are voices internally within our own lives of, fear, rational thinking and erratic feelings, all capable of bringing restriction and robbing us of God's best.

The most powerful and dangerous voice of all though, is the **Voice of Deception**, trying to bring confusion into our lives and lead us out of God's will. We are without doubt living in the 'last days' and the Bible says that in these times there will be a wide spread of deception and an increase of false prophets. God's word gives us a serious warning in this regard. It says,

> 'Beware of false prophets, who come to you in sheep's clothing but inwardly are ravenous wolves.'
>
> (Matthew 7:15)

Then in Acts 20:30 (NIV) we read,

> 'Even from your own number men will arise and distort the truth in order to draw away disciples after them.'

And also in 1 John 4:1 it says,

> 'Beloved, do not believe every spirit, but test the spirits to see whether they are of God; for many false prophets have gone out into the world.'

There are many people going around today causing havoc in the lives of others, by giving them so called 'prophetic words' of direction. Although God does speak in such ways, this should generally only be taken to confirm what the Lord has already been saying to us, and not our sole means of guidance.

I well remember an incident that happened to me 16 years ago when I was praying for God's direction. I needed the Lord to show me the right time to leave my secular employment as a salesman, and where to step out into full-time Christian service. One evening I went along to a presentation by the 'Youth With A Mission' organisation in Exeter. The venue was full with about four hundred people. I wasn't in the building for more that a few minutes when someone I'd never met before from the YWAM team, left the platform and came straight to me at the back of the hall. With great conviction the person said, 'The Lord has shown me you're to join the team and come with us to America!' Encouraged by this I went away and prayed about the matter. Then shared it with others and looked for further confirmation, but it became obvious that God was not leading me to go off to America. Now if I'd just made a decision and gone on this so-called 'Word from the Lord', it could have had disastrous consequences.

The voice of deception infiltrates our lives not just via 'prophetic words', but also through teaching which is a mixture of truth and error. One of the important things I believe God is saying today is that we need to realise the nature of the deception that is coming in these end times. It is not going to be spoken merely from the 'oddballs' and 'cranks' of this world. Let's face it, you don't need a lot of discernment to know if it's God's word when someone a little strange speaks out! The deception we need to be on our guard against is going to be coming from sincere, anointed, respected, charismatic men of God. Leaders and preachers that are well known names! This is how the 'Heavy Shepherding, Submission Movement' spread across this country, not through 'oddballs', but men of God that we all know and respect. Also some extremes in faith and prosperity teaching, inner healing and extreme deliverance teaching have come into our churches, not through 'cranks', but godly men. Even in recent times, established charismatic leaders and solid evangelical names have been denying the literal biblical view of hell. Instead they have taught their own ideas on annihilation, which are totally contrary to Scripture.

We must take great care not to swallow anything and everything that a leading figure has said, just because of his or her reputation. Rather the Bible says,

> 'do not despise prophesying, but test everything; hold fast what is good.' (1 Thessalonians 5:20 & 21)

In our own life-time we are seeing come to pass the scripture that says,

> 'For the time is coming when people will not endure sound teaching, but having itching ears they will

> *accumulate for themselves teachers to suit their own*
> *likings, and will turn away from listening to the truth*
> *and wander into myths.'*   (2 Timothy 4:3 & 4)

The great challenge for us is that the Lord expects every Christian to recognise His voice, over and above all these other voices. In fact it would be true to say that one of the evidences of being a genuine disciple is that we are able to do so. Jesus made this clear in saying,

> *'My sheep hear my voice, and I know them, and they*
> *follow me.'*   (John 10:27)

We cannot be truly walking with the Lord unless this is evident in our lives, no matter how sincere we may be.

How to be Sure About Guidance

Let us now consider some practical steps to follow that will help us be sure of walking in God's will, so that the right decisions are made when the occasion demands.

Firstly – *Faith is the Basis on which we Begin*

How often we forget to pray about everyday decisions! Choices are made without any expression of faith in our dependency on God. We make them with confidence in ourselves, on the spur of the moment, without enquiring of the Lord, then wonder why the end result is unsatisfactory.

In the Bible, nearly a whole generation of God's people took forty years to make a journey which should have only taken eleven days! They wandered around in the wilderness, never entering the promised provision of God. The reason why is given in Hebrews 3:19;

> *'So we see that they were unable to enter because of*
> *unbelief.'*

117

We must have faith that God has a plan for our lives and wants to reveal this to us. Faith also that as sovereign Lord He is able even to overrule in our circumstances. The Bible says,

> *'What he opens, no-one can shut; and what he shuts, no-one can open.'*   (Revelation 3:7b, NIV)

As we believe His promises and walk in faith, our way will be made clear. This is why Solomon wrote,

> *'Trust in the Lord with all your heart, and do not rely on your own insight. In all your ways acknowledge him, and he will make straight your paths.'*
> (Proverbs 3:5 & 6)

It is possible to get a computer program today, that will give you the quickest, most direct route for travelling to any destination. As Christians also, God doesn't want us to be going around in a wilderness of uncertainty getting nowhere in our lives. He is able to show us the most direct route if we will start on the basis of faith, believing that He will guide our paths. The Bible assures us of this when it says,

> *'The steps of a good man are ordered by the Lord . . .'*
> (Psalm 37:23, AV)

Faith in God's leading, especially during times of trouble, is found in the example of the famous hymn writer, Fanny Crosby. When she was only six weeks old her doctors made a tragic mistake by putting the wrong eye drops in her eyes, causing her to be blind for the rest of her life. As she grew up she committed herself to Christ and found in Jesus the perfect guide. In her world of darkness she wrote thousands of hymns, but amongst them, one of the best known speaks of her faith in the Lord's guidance. Part of it says:

'All the way my Saviour leads me:
What have I to ask beside?
Can I doubt His tender mercy,
Who through life has been my Guide?
Heavenly peace divinest comfort,
Here by faith in Him to dwell!
For I know whate'er befall me,
Jesus doeth all things well.'

Secondly – *Maintain a Close Relationship with God*

Relationship is the key to recognising who it is that is speaking. When I travel away for 17 days every month on itinerary, I always make a point of ringing each day to speak to my wife and children. Invariably one of my young daughters will be first to pick up the phone. When they do, I don't have to formally introduce myself to them, all that is needed is for me to speak one word, and instantly they know that it's 'daddy!' From out of our relationship they are able to recognise straight away who is speaking, and so it should be with our Heavenly Father.

In Exodus 33:11 we read,

> *'Thus the Lord used to speak to Moses face to face, as a man speaks to his friend . . .'* (Exodus 33:11)

When Jesus was making this point of relationship to his disciples He said,

> *'No longer do I call you servants, for the servant does not know what his master is doing; but I have called you friends, for all that I have heard from my Father I have made known to you.'* (John 15:15)

Some people only speak to God as a last resort, perhaps as they would the Samaritans, at a time of crisis, or maybe like they'd turn to the Citizens Advice Bureau for help. The Bible however says,

'In all your ways acknowledge him, and he will make straight your paths.' (Proverbs 3:6)

Revelation comes out of relationship. This is absolutely fundamental if we're to be clear about the Lord's will. To be able to hear God's voice we must take care to be in tune with Him. Consider the illustration of a radio. If that is not precisely in tune, then the message coming across will be distorted and it will be difficult to make sense of it; we could even misunderstand what is being communicated.

For this friendship to be developed with God we need to make sure that in the busyness of our lives we are taking time to stop and listen. The French physicist, mathematician and philosopher Blaise Pascal once said,

> 'Nearly all of the ills in our life spring from this one simple source, that we are not able to sit still in a room.'

Deliberately giving time and opportunity to be still enables our relationship to grow and we become more aware of God. This is why the Lord instructs us in Psalm 46:10,

'Be still, and know that I am God . . . '

Thirdly – *Be Diligent in God's Word*

It was the well known author and teacher Dr A.W. Tozer who said,

> '95% of God's will for our life is already revealed in the Bible.'

When we are doing what God has already made known then other areas that aren't so black and white become much clearer. This I believe is one of the major keys to guidance for every Christian. There can be no substitute to feeding daily upon the scriptures. Knowing our Bibles well is the best safeguard against deception, because

120

God's will for our lives will never contradict His word. This is why Jesus said,

> *'Man shall not live by bread alone, but by every word that proceeds from the mouth of God.'*   (Matthew 4:4)

If we value and honour God's word, seeing it as having vital importance to the well being of our lives, then we will discipline ourselves to give time to feeding upon what God says.

George Muller was an outstanding man of faith who accomplished so much as he walked in God's will. He understood only too well the importance of this discipline. Having read through the Bible one hundred times he made this statement:

> 'I look upon it as a lost day when I have not had a good time over the word of God. Friends say, "I have so much to do, so many people to see, I cannot find time for scripture study." Perhaps there are not many who have more to do than I. For more than half a century I have never known one day when I had not more business than I could get through. For four years I have had annually about thirty thousand letters, and most of these have passed through my own hands. Then, as pastor of a church with twelve hundred believers, great has been my care. Besides, I have had charge of five immense orphanages; also, at my publishing depot, the printing and circulating of millions of tracts, books and Bibles; but I have always made it a rule never to begin work until I have had a good season with God and His word.'

In the darkness and uncertainties of life today we can see the relevance of what the Psalmist meant when he said,

> *'Thy Word is a lamp to my feet and light to my path.'*
> (Psalm 119:105)

Fourthly – *Seek the Counsel of Others*

One of the most common reasons why people fall into
deception and end up creating needless pain for themselves and those around them, is that they are unteach-
able. We all need to look to the wisdom of others,
especially on major decisions. I've had the experience
countless times, of Christians coming to me saying, 'The
Lord has told me to do . . . ' When I ask them if they have
sought the advice of others they look at me as though I'm
from a different planet! Then a few weeks later what they
felt 'led' into has either collapsed or they feel 'led' again,
but in a different direction. This sort of living is not glor-
ifying to the Lord. It is also in direct contradiction to His
Word which says,

> *'Listen to advice and accept instruction, that you may
> gain wisdom for the future.'* (Proverbs 19:20)

One Christian lady recently came to encourage us as we
were preaching in the town centre of Leicester. When I
asked what church she belonged to she said, 'Oh I don't
go anywhere at the moment. The Lord has told me that
I've got to have a year's sabbatical from the church. In
fact God has shown me to have one year off in every
seven!' No amount of persuasion would convince her that
this was contrary to God's word. She rejected all we said
with the firm rebuff, 'Well the Lord has told me and that's
the end of the matter!'

Another lady from Kent who was always declaring,
'The Lord has told me . . . ', just wouldn't accept any counsel that was contrary to what she had set her mind to do.
Having been divorced twice she met another man and after
knowing him for only two weeks they were married. She
rejected all advice for caution by saying, **'The Lord has
told me it is His will.'** Sadly, soon after their wedding the
relationship ended in tears!

Almost always, three main things stop people looking to
the counsel of others.

(a) *Independence* – the attitude, 'It's just me and Jesus, all I need is the Lord!'

(b) *Insecurity* – the fear of someone saying what we don't want to hear, and

(c) *Pride* – not wanting others to know that we need help.

The Bible however, makes it very clear how important other people are in the guidance of our lives. It says,

> *'In the abundance of counsellors there is safety.'*
> (Proverbs 11:14b)

And again in Proverbs 15:22,

> *'Without counsel plans go wrong, but with many advisers they succeed.'*

The benefit of having the view of an experienced helper is well illustrated by something I heard recently. Apparently at Hampton Court Palace near London, there is a maze in which visitors regularly get lost. At closing time the keeper brings out some tall platform steps and climbs to the top. From this high vantage point he can see the whole picture and directs people to the exit. This is just the same with those in the middle of puzzling circumstances. They can feel lost and confused by being so close to the situation, but someone looking on from a more objective perspective can give the clear guidance that is necessary.

Fifthly – *Have a Genuine Desire to do God's Will*

It is I believe, difficult to miss the will of God if we really want to do it. This is why there must be more than an interest to **'know'** God's guidance. A readiness to **'Do'** God's will, whatever it might be, is essential. The counsel of Mary to the servants when they were in need of direction was, *'Do whatever he tells you'* (John 2:5b). God looks for that willing, unconditional surrender to do whatever He might say. Not, 'Lord show me, then I'll decide,' but an attitude, when the Lord says 'Jump!' – you jump and on the way up ask, 'How high Lord!'

As we surrender our wills to Him and present our lives in purity, we place ourselves in the position of being able to discover His purpose. Paul puts it like this,

> *'I appeal to you therefore, brethren, by the mercies of God, to present your bodies as a living sacrifice, holy and acceptable to God, which is your spiritual worship . . . that you might prove what is the will of God, what is good and acceptable and perfect.'* (Romans 12:1 & 2)

In the life of Jesus we see His passion to do God's will regardless of the cost. He could say,

> *'My food is to do the will of him who sent me, and to accomplish his work.'* (John 4:34)

What is necessary is not the 'eventual obedience' of someone like Jonah who at first ran away from God's clear direction. Nor, 'reluctant obedience' as is found at times in the lives of Christians who take on God given tasks, but not with glad and willing service. The Lord looks for 'immediate obedience'. A genuine desire to do His will even when it might be difficult and require sacrifice. Sometimes our own desires can get in the way of God's will for our lives and at such times we need to look to the example of Jesus. He could say in the Garden of Gethsemane, when considering the cost of obedience in relation to the cross,

> *'My Father, if it is possible, may this cup be taken from me. Yet not as I will, but as you will.'*
> (Matthew 26:39, NIV)

Sixthly – *Listen for that Inner Witness*
God is able to speak to His children in an audible voice to

reveal some matter to them. Generally however, it is by means of that still, inner voice that He speaks to our spirit. By prompting, leading, directing and influencing, or at times checking us from taking some undesirable course of action God guides our lives.

What we're talking about here is an 'inner knowing' that can be understood in two ways.

(a) There are those times when we have a peace within, about a particular step we've taken, or perhaps the loss of that peace when a wrong decision has been made. Then we feel unsettled, uneasy or restless about a certain course of action. This is what the Bible means when it says,

> *'Let the peace of Christ rule in your heart . . .'*
> (Colossians 3:15)

The literal meaning of the word 'rule' in the Greek is to 'umpire' or make the final decision. This leading of peace as an inner witness, keeping us in the will of God, is seen also when Paul wrote,

> *'The peace of God, which passes all understanding, will keep your hearts and your minds in Christ Jesus.'*
> (Philippians 4:7)

(b) The other kind of witness is a strong inner conviction that moves us to action! As God's word comes there is no doubt who it is that is speaking and what we must do. The most unlikely people were given this strong conviction to step out in faith. Matthew was a despised tax collector but we read of him,

> *'As Jesus passed on from there, he saw a man called Matthew sitting at the tax office; and he said to him, "Follow me." And he rose and followed him.'*
> (Matthew 9:9)

Also Jesus spoke to a band of fishermen and called them to be His disciples. Their response was to leave their nets, boats and family and immediately follow after Him (Mark 1:17–20). Again when reading about the woman of Samaria, we find that the conviction she felt was so strong she immediately left her water jar, ran back to her village and proclaimed,

> *'Come, see a man that told me all that I ever did.'*
>
> (John 4:29)

The same conviction has motivated others throughout Church history and still does today. For example, William Carey was an ordinary shoe-maker working in Northampton, but one day the call of God came to him to go to India. He had a deep inner conviction to translate the Bible into the languages of the people. As a result, his many labours included founding the Baptist Missionary Society in 1792 and eventually translating the complete Bible into Bengali, and its translation, in whole or part into twenty four other languages and dialects. Throughout his work he experienced much sorrow, hardship and many disappointments. This God-given conviction though, enabled him to continue through it all and kept him obedient to God's will.

Gladys Aylward was another who responded to God's leading in this way. Born in Edmonton, North London in 1902 she worked as a simple parlour maid. One day a strong conviction told her that she was to go to China and serve the Lord in that land. With enthusiasm she went to the missionary society to make herself available, but they turned her down. In their eyes she was unqualified and too weak to be a missionary. This set-back didn't stop her or diminish in any way what she knew God had called her to. So without any help from the society, she got on board a train in 1932, went to China and for 17 years accomplished a tremendous work for the Lord in that land!

God has promised to guide our lives but it is our

responsibility to seek His direction. He is only too ready to reveal His will for each one of us. We must look carefully and prayerfully to the various steps that have been mentioned for confirmation. Not taking any one of them on their own, nor expecting to find them all, but as a safeguard looking to as many of these as possible. In doing so with a sincere and willing heart, we can find guidance in uncertainty.

Chapter 8

Guarding Against Pollution

There is great alarm and talk today, concerning the poison of pollution, that can be found all around us in life. We seem to hear warnings regularly about the dangers of the seas we swim in, the air that we breathe, the water we drink, and even the food that we eat. A few years ago, our family was made very aware of this problem. Over a period of just twelve months, we discovered a sliver of glass in a hamburger, a 1½ inch dress pin in a jam doughnut, a dead wasp in a can of beans, some broken glass in a packet of crisps and a frozen chicken that when defrosted for our Sunday lunch, had turned green and started to smell!

In looking at this subject of 'Guarding Against Pollution', there is something even more common and dangerous, than might immediately spring to mind. The purpose of this chapter is not to raise people's consciousness concerning our environment, important though that is. What we are considering here, is not a 'Green Issue', but a serious spiritual problem, that affects every one of us. The most dangerous pollutant, which can contaminate and poison the quality of life, is already in our bodies, right now!

God's word alerts each of us to this danger in James 3:2–10. Here we are warned about the power of the tongue. The one muscle in our body that receives more exercise and less control than any other. It is pictured by James as a *'Destructive Fire'*, capable of devastating everything in its path.

> *'So the tongue is a little member and boasts of great things. How great a forest is set ablaze by a small fire! And the tongue is a fire...'* (James 3:5 & 6)

A tiny spark smaller than a finger nail, holds the power to destroy thousands of acres of forest. Likewise the tongue, though relatively small, can create havoc far beyond its apparent size.

James also speaks of it as a *'Deadly Poison'* (verse 8b), contaminating and killing all with which it comes into contact. The whole world of evil can find its expression through the tongue. Boastful pride, destructive anger, cutting bitterness, flattering lust etc. Something of the full extent of this restless, poisonous evil, was heard when Hitler unleashed his tongue against Christianity. In a mindless rage, as a man possessed, he said,

> 'Nothing will prevent me from tearing up Christianity, root and branch ... we are not against a hundred and one different kinds of Christianity, but against Christianity itself. All people who profess creeds are traitors to the people. Even those Christians who really want to serve others we have to suppress. I myself am a heathen to the core!'

The tongue is then spoken of as a *'Deceptive Power'*, enabling us to communicate with God in one breath but also crush His creation in the next.

> *'With it we bless the Lord and Father, and with it we curse men, who are made in the likeness of God.'*
> (James 3:9)

This is probably hypocrisy and self-deception at its worst.

With the same tongue can come blessing and cursing. The awful thing is that people can appear so spiritual one moment, then the next, actually be cursing those around them for whom Christ died.

These three things are not a very nice description, but we've all got the potential of them in our mouths! It's important to underline the fact that James is clearly speaking to Christians about this problem and not those outside the Church. In writing to believers he cries out with exasperation, *'My brethren, this ought not to be so'* (verse 10b). Jesus also spoke to His followers about the responsibility to take care regarding what is said. He stated,

> *'But I tell you that men will have to give account on the day of judgment for every careless word they have spoken. For by your words you will be acquitted, and by your words you will be condemned.'*
> (Matthew 12:36 & 37, NIV)

The Bible consistently gives a clear warning about the tongue and shows that we need to be on our guard because of its danger. In Proverbs 10:19 we read,

> *'When words are many, sin is not absent...'* (NIV)

What this verse says in effect is, the more words we speak, the more likely sin will be present! If for any length of time we find ourselves just sitting around chatting with others, it won't be long before sin enters into the conversation. We might have had a wonderful Sunday morning meeting and known the blessing of God in that service. Then when we come home and have time to relax, just talking, quite often something sinful will creep in to what is being said. At the very least, 'Roast Preacher' will be on the menu in many households come lunch time!

We each have the choice of using our tongue in a constructive or destructive way. This is what the Bible means when it says,

131

> *'Death and life are in the power of the tongue . . .'*
> (Proverbs 18:21)

The words we speak can either build up, strengthen and be the means of bringing life in situations that are dead, or alternatively they can break down and destroy, bringing death into situations of life.

Constructive Words of Life

The example of Jesus illustrates how by words, life can be imparted into circumstances that appear dead and beyond change. At every opportunity when Jesus spoke, His aim was to transform the very atmosphere of hopelessness that people were in. Even while suffering in great agony on the cross, words of blessing came from His lips towards others.

Throughout His ministry we find that this was very much the case. Against demonic powers of oppression, torment and bondage the Bible tells us,

> *'he drove out the spirits **with a word** . . .'*
> (Matthew 8:16b, NIV)

With sickness, the request from a Centurion for Jesus to heal his servant was,

> *'Speak the word only, and my servant shall be healed.'*
> (Matthew 8:8b, AV)

When two weary disciples walked down the Emma'us road, they reflected on their earlier conversation with Jesus and said,

> *'Did not our hearts burn within us while he talked to us on the road . . .'* (Luke 24:32)

132

The words Jesus expressed made an impact on everyone, which is why people remarked in astonishment,

> *'No man ever spoke like this man!'* (John 7:46b)

The incredible thing is, Jesus taught that we too, by the words we speak, should have that same power to impart life and blessing to others. By walking in the power of the Holy Spirit and being sensitive to His will and direction, God's word in our mouth can have the same power as God's word in God's mouth!

This astonishing teaching is brought out in Mark 11:12–21. Here we read how Jesus had just rebuked a fig tree because it bore no fruit. When the disciples passed by that same place the following day, they noticed that it had withered completely, from the root. Noticing their surprise Jesus then says, (in the same context of the effect of His word upon the fig tree),

> *'Truly, I say to you, whoever says to this mountain, "Be taken up and cast into the sea," and does not doubt in his heart, but believes that what he says will come to pass, it will be done for him.'* (Mark 11:23)

The extent of this potential to make the same impact as Jesus is reinforced when He said,

> *'Truly, truly, I say unto you, he who believes in me will also do the works that I do; and greater works than these will he do, because I go to the Father.'*
> (John 14:12)

Furthermore, we find again the expectation of this in John's Epistle when the Apostle wrote,

> *'He who says he abides in him ought to walk in the same way in which he walked.'* (1 John 2:6)

The book of Acts shows us how this teaching was applied as the disciples took Jesus literally. They started to speak into areas of need, bringing the life and blessing of God to others. For example, Peter met a man who had been lame for forty years. He responded to the problem by speaking the word of healing into the pollution of sickness, just as he'd been taught to do. He said,

> *'I have no silver and gold, but I give you what I have; in the name of Jesus Christ of Nazareth, walk.'*
>
> (Acts 3:6)

No long prayer was used, simply the power of the spoken word and the result was that instantly healing came into that lame man's body.

Then Peter came to a village called Lydda and found a man named Aene'as who was paralysed and had been bed-ridden for eight years. Help was brought into this person's need by the spoken word. Peter said to the man,

> *'Aene'as, Jesus Christ heals you; rise and make your bed. And immediately he rose.'*   (Acts 9:34)

In the same chapter we see the power of the spoken word actually bringing life into a dead body. At Joppa a disciple named Tabitha had died and Peter spoke against death, just as Jesus had done with Lazarus, and commanded life to come back into her. He said, *'Tabitha, rise.'* And the result was, *'she opened her eyes, and when she saw Peter she sat up'* (Acts 9:40b).

We also find the amazing effect of words that are anointed by the Holy Spirit in the ministry of Paul, when he was being opposed by a magician called El'ymas. The Bible says,

> *'But Saul, who is also called Paul, filled with the Holy Spirit, looked intently at him and said "You son of the devil, you enemy of all righteousness, full of deceit and*

134

villain, will you not stop making crooked the straight paths of the Lord? And now, behold, the hand of the Lord is upon you, and you shall be blind and unable to see the sun for a time." Immediately mist and darkness fell upon him and he went about seeking people to lead him by the hand.' (Acts 13:9–11)

One other example of how the tongue can be used powerfully not only to guard against the pollution of evil, but actively bring the life of God to people, is seen again in Paul's ministry at a place called Lystra. Here was a man who had been crippled from birth. He was listening to the Apostle speaking when suddenly Paul looked intently at him and in a loud voice said, *'Stand upright on your feet.'* The Bible then tells us, *'he sprang up and walked'* (Acts 14:10).

Destructive Words of Death

While the tongue can be used constructively and was always intended by God to bring life and blessing to others, more often than not this fails to be the case. All too frequently words are spoken that are destructive and which pollute the atmosphere of faith, harmfully affecting those around us. Let us consider some of the ways that this can happen.

Firstly – *Negative Talk*
This flows out of those that tend to see and expect the worst in people and situations. Their words express an attitude of doubt, despair and unbelief. They normally focus on the problem and communicate a sense of hopelessness. The actual words themselves might be factually correct, but the negative attitude in which they are spoken can have a damaging influence on those who hear. Speaking such words could undermine the faith of others and bring insecurity, uncertainty and fear into their lives. This is particularly so in the relationships of those we

135

frequently come into contact with, like our marriage partner, children, or fellow church members.

The effect of negative talk is illustrated by the report that the twelve spies brought back from the promised land. Ten of the twelve returned speaking of the people being strong, the cities well fortified and the notorious descendants of Anak being present. While their facts were correct, the Bible says, they brought back an *'evil report'* (Numbers 13:32). This was so, not because it was untrue they had spoken of what they had seen. It was an evil report because of their defeatist attitude in saying,

> *'We are not able to go up against the people; for they are stronger than we.'*   (Numbers 13:31)

Also it was evil because of the effect Joshua tells us it had upon all who heard them. He said,

> *'My brethren who went up with me made the heart of the people melt . . .'*   (Joshua 14:8)

The only two that came back with a positive attitude were Joshua and Caleb. They had seen exactly the same things as the other ten but their response was,

> *'let us go up at once, and occupy it; for we are well able to overcome it.'*   (Numbers 13:30)

Secondly – *Criticism and Gossip*
One amusing definition of a real Christian is, 'Someone who can give his pet parrot to the town gossip!' Not many I would imagine, could have that confidence regarding their conversation. When criticism is not constructive, not spoken in genuine love and hasn't the ultimate good of the other person at heart, it is sin and easily picked up and repeated. Someone with a critical spirit will often begin by grumbling, complaining, and finding fault. Then as we mentioned in the chapter on resentment, their words can

136

even develop into 'character assassination'. Simply the tone of voice that is used in conversation, or the subtle innuendo expressed, can communicate something that is able to damage the reputation and character of another. The old maxim is very true,

> 'If you can't say anything good about a person, it's best to say nothing at all.'

Hand in hand with criticism goes gossip. This can take a very 'super spiritual' guise as someone says, 'I'm just telling you this so that you can pray about the situation.' If we pass on anything that we know the person we are talking about would not be happy with, then this is nothing short of sinful gossip! Such things can bring discord into the Church and damage general relationships. The Bible is very clear on how God feels about this when His word says,

> *'There are six things the Lord hates, seven which are an abomination to him . . . a man who sows discord among brothers.'* (Proverbs 6:16–19)

Again we read about the effect of these words and an indication of the type of person that speaks them in Proverbs 16:28,

> *'A perverse man spreads strife, and a whisperer separates close friends.'*

Thirdly – *Sarcasm and Flippant Humour*
American Evangelist Billy Graham once said,

> 'A keen sense of humour helps us to overlook the unbecoming, understand the unconventional, tolerate the unpleasant, overcome the unexpected and outlast the unbearable!'

137

God wants us to have a sense of humour. To be able to laugh,.. particularly at ourselves, is very important. Humour is a healthy, natural and attractive quality within our personality.

Having said this though, we need to be on our guard at the way the enemy gets in here and spoils this wonderful God-given gift. The abuse of humour can wound and hurt others. Through some flippant remark or sarcastic comment, a person's confidence can be shattered, self-doubt sown and offence caused. It's often said that, 'Sarcasm is the lowest form of wit.' **Sarcasm is not wit, it is sin**, because of the effect it can have upon the lives of others. This is why Paul wrote to the Church at Ephesus and said,

> 'Let there be no filthiness, nor silly talk, nor levity, which are not fitting...' (Ephesians 5:4)

Sometimes people try to cover up the offence that their remark has caused by saying, 'I was only joking!' Whether this excuse be true or not, there is still no way of justifying the hurt that has occurred through a flippant, thoughtless comment at someone else's expense. The Bible shows graphically the seriousness of this sort of thing when it says,

> 'like a madman who throws firebrands, arrows, and death, is the man who deceives his neighbour and says, "I was only joking!"' (Proverbs 26:18 & 19)

Fourthly – *Controversy and Disputes*

In the New Testament we see this was a problem that Paul had to address when he wrote to the Galatian church. To them he said,

> 'You shall love your neighbours as you love yourself. But if you bite and devour one another take heed that you are not consumed by one another.'
> (Galatians 5:14–16)

I'm told that if a rattlesnake is cornered, it can become so frenzied that it will accidently bite itself with its deadly fangs. In the same way, when people become contentious, they not only hurt those around them, but also they are unwittingly inflicting deep harm within their own souls.

It's sad but true that often the greatest hurts we experience are not caused by the attitudes of unconverted people in the world, but by other Christians in the church! In travelling throughout the country ministering, I find this biting and devouring of one another is unfortunately so common. People fall out over the smallest things. Grudges are held, relationships broken and the church is split over something that might in itself be very insignificant. I've been to places where there has been contention and division ranging from the fabric of the building, to the finer points of belief!

The result of controversy and disputes is a loss of peace, disunity and ultimately bondage. It is something that very often comes from spiritual pride and was a problem in the New Testament Church, just like it is today. This is why the Bible has much to say in warning us to be on our guard about the way it can pollute the atmosphere of faith and unity. In 1 Timothy 6:4 & 5 we read,

> '... puffed up with conceit, he knows nothing; he has a morbid craving for controversy and for disputes about words, which produce envy, dissension, slander, base suspicions, and wrangling among men ... '

Also in 2 Timothy 2:14 Paul says,

> 'Remind them of this, and charge them before the Lord to avoid disputing about words, which does no good, but only ruins the hearers.'

Another revealing scripture is found in Titus 3:9. The instruction here is,

139

'But avoid stupid controversies, genealogies, dissensions and quarrels over the law, for they are unprofitable and futile.'

Fifthly – *Lying*

Here is one word that is not popular to mention in polite circles. Politicians have tried to dress it up and make it seem less serious, even light hearted, calling it, 'being economical with the truth!' Whichever way it is referred to though, any departure from the full truth is lying. While this is accepted as a problem with some in society, it seems almost an affront to suggest it is widespread also in the Church. However, even Christians can be guilty of allowing their tongues to be used in such a way.

The Bible takes a strong stand against such abuse of the tongue, leaving us in no doubt as to how God feels about it. In the Old Testament we read,

'Lying lips are an abomination to the Lord . . . '
(Proverbs 12:22)

Also in the New Testament, Paul had to confront the problem when he spoke to the Colossian Church. His instruction to the believers there was,

'Do not lie to one another, seeing that you have put off the old nature with its practices.' (Colossians 3:9)

Often with Christians, the 'big' blatant lies are not so common. More frequently it is words expressed in a less obvious way, but they are just as serious. For example, communicating 'half truths', where we knowingly withhold part of the truth for our own advantage. Maybe occasions where we misrepresent or manipulate the facts to deliberately give a false impression. This could include the way our tax returns are filled in. Insurance claims that are made, submitting a report at work, applying for a job or simply recounting an incident that has happened to us.

Another area is exaggeration in the things we say, to make ourselves look good. This again is a departure from the truth. Also even when we express false modesty, saying we're not able to do something when really we are quite capable, what we are actually doing is lying. If we are not straightforward with the truth in any way, then in reality we are attempting to deceive.

The Root of the Problem

As with all of the problem areas in these chapters there is obviously a root cause. This needs to be established so that we might be on our guard against what we could say with our tongues.

(a) The main root of the problem is the state and condition of our own hearts. Jesus taught,

> *'For out of the abundance of the heart the mouth speaks.'* (Matthew 12:34b)

It is an interesting fact that if we listen long enough to a person's conversation, eventually what they say will betray them. This is particularly so outside the church meeting and is evident either when people are under pressure with problems, or they are relaxed and off guard. What is in their heart will eventually come out on their tongue. We therefore begin to see where a person is spiritually, just by listening carefully to what they are saying. With this in mind King Solomon wrote,

> *'Even a fool who keeps silent is considered wise; when he closes his lips, he is deemed intelligent.'* (Proverbs 17:28)

This is why our relationship with the Lord is a major factor in affecting the things we say. A heart filled with Christ will reveal His nature in all circumstances. The expression of a Christ-like character will be evident in how we speak and react to others. Paul writes of this in 1 Corinthians 13:4–7:

> '*Love is patient and kind; love is not jealous or boastful; it is not arrogant or rude. Love does not insist on its own way; it is not irritable or resentful; it does not rejoice at wrong, but rejoices in the right. Love bears all things, believes all things, hopes all things, endures all things.*'

The opposite of these qualities will of course be the case, if we have not got that right relationship with the Lord.

(b) Our attitudes are shaped in the early years of our life and play a large part in the things we say as adults today. I'm sure we've all had the experience of hearing ourselves say something, then afterwards thinking, 'That's just what my father used to say' or, 'That's exactly how my mother always used to respond.' The example of role models such as parents, teachers and friends have a significant impact upon us and leave a deep impression, even many years later. If those around us as we were growing up have been negative, critical, harsh, argumentative, sarcastic etc. subconsciously as children we soon pick it up. It has been said:

> 'If a child lives with criticism, He learns to condemn.
> If a child lives with hostility, He learns to fight.
> If a child lives with ridicule, He learns to be shy.
> If a child lives with shame, He learns to feel guilty.
> If a child lives with tolerance, He learns to be patient.
> If a child lives with encouragement, He learns confidence.
> If a child lives with praise, He learns to appreciate.
> If a child lives with fairness, He learns justice.
> If a child lives with security, He learns to have faith.

If a child lives with approval, He learns to like
    himself.
If a child lives with acceptance and friendship, He
    learns to find love in the world.'

(c)   We must also take into account and never minimise the way that demonic powers can take advantage of
someone who isn't fully surrendered to the Lord. Those
with unconfessed sin in their lives, who hold grudges
against others, are discontented and have unrighteous attitudes etc. leave themselves wide open to be manipulated
by satanic powers. It is through such people that the
works of darkness can have a 'field day' in a church and
also wreak havoc in the lives of individuals. Through
words prompted by the enemy; deception, doubt, discouragement and disunity quickly come in, affecting the
vibrant life and blessing of all that they touch. This root
cause is exposed by James as he says the tongue is, '... *set
on fire by hell*' (James 3:6b), and also that it is, '... *a restless evil* ... ' (James 3:8b).

Where the Answer is Found

Praise God there is an answer to such a serious problem
and that answer is found by all who desire to know victory
in this area. Three steps applied by faith, can bring change
that will transform the tongue from being a **Destructive
Problem**, to a **Constructive Power!**

Firstly – *Conviction*
Here is where the answer begins. There can be no short cut
or by-passing this important need if we are to truly guard
against the danger of our tongues. God's Holy Spirit
bringing 'old fashioned' conviction is the only way change
comes. This is the same conviction that we read about on
the day of Pentecost as people became aware of their sin.
They didn't make excuses or try to rationalise their situation, rather we read,

143

'... they were cut to the heart, and said to Peter and the rest of the apostles, "Brethren, what shall we do?"'
(Acts 2:37)

It's by having a revelation of who the Lord is, and seeing the standard of His holiness that we become acutely aware of how far we fall short. Then we are motivated to do something to change. This does not leave us in a state of condemnation, but brings us to a place of urgency to get right with God. We see such an example in the life of the prophet Isaiah. He was holding office in the temple, representing God to the people but there came an occasion when great conviction was brought to him regarding his tongue.

Isaiah recalled this experience as he wrote,

> *'In the year that King Uzzi'ah died I saw the Lord sitting upon a throne, high and lifted up; and his train filled the temple. Above him stood the seraphim; each had six wings: with two he covered his face, and with two he covered his feet, and with two he flew. And one called to another and said: "Holy, holy, holy is the Lord of hosts; the whole earth is full of his glory." And the foundations of the thresholds shook at the voice of him who called, and the house was filled with smoke. And I said: "Woe is me! For I am lost; for **I am a man of unclean lips, and I dwell in the midst of a people of unclean lips**; for my eyes have seen the King, the Lord of hosts!"'*
> (Isaiah 6:1–5)

The encouraging thing that we find further on in this passage is that God didn't cast him aside. Once his lips were cleansed the Lord sent him out with a new and mighty ministry to use his tongue in service for God (verses 6–13).

Secondly – *Commitment*
Having been convicted and received forgiveness for our

sin, we need to make a commitment for Jesus to be Lord of every area of our lives, especially our tongues. The genuineness of our response will be seen in an earnest desire for righteousness to be in all that we say. When Job had much to be negative about because of the difficult circumstances he was in, his commitment was expressed in the words,

> *'My lips will not speak falsehood, and my tongue will not utter deceit.'* (Job 27:4)

We must refuse to allow our tongue to be used for the devil's work! In making this commitment, we are settling in our hearts to speak only 'faith filled' words that will build up, strengthen, restore and bless. Careful use of our tongue can bring healing into lives that are damaged. The Bible says,

> *'. . . rash words are like sword thrusts, but the tongue of the wise brings healing.'* (Proverbs 12:18)

The extent of this commitment and its effect is spelt out by Paul when he wrote to the Church at Ephesus. He said,

> *'Let no evil talk come out of your mouths, but only such as is good for edifying, as fits the occasion, that it might impart grace to those who hear.'*
> (Ephesians 4:29)

What a wonderful thought that when we have this resolve, then each time we speak to others, we are able to impart grace to those who are listening.

This commitment must be worked out practically in our daily lives. For example, when we find ourselves in an unrighteous atmosphere where the conversation is negative, critical or ungodly in any way, then we have a responsibility to do something about it. Sometimes it will be necessary to take a stand and speak out, correcting what is being said. In other situations it might be more

145

appropriate to simply re-direct the conversation that is getting negative, by saying something positive. In some instances, perhaps simply to withdraw from what is being spoken about would be the right action.

Listening to unrighteous talk and doing nothing, is as bad as being a part of what has been said and we will soon get drawn in and polluted by it. I well remember in a team situation some years ago, sitting around a table with about a dozen other men who were in ministry. The conversation started to get very critical about a person who wasn't present in the room. The discussion became so unrighteous that I took a stand, and stated that I believed what was being said was sinful, and I wanted no part of it. Although there was a stunned, embarrassed silence, the discussion quickly returned to matters which were more wholesome.

In our commitment to do something when finding ourselves in such a position, it's very important that we don't get paranoid and 'super spiritual'. We must take care not to be jumping heavily on everything and everyone the moment a slip of the tongue is made. When speaking out we need to do so with sensitivity, wisdom and humility.

Thirdly – *Control*
To be disciplined in what we say through our own strength is impossible. James points this out by saying,

> *'No human being can tame the tongue...'*
>
> (James 3:8)

We will soon be disappointed in our desire to be victorious in this area, if we fail to see the importance of being filled with the Holy Spirit. It is only by God's indwelling power that we can possibly maintain our position and have an influence on others. When we are seeking daily to live 'Spirit filled' lives, then the effect of God's Spirit upon what we say is quite dramatic. This is something we can see in the scripture which says,

146

> *'But the fruit of the spirit is love, joy, peace, patience, kindness, goodness, faithfulness gentleness, self-control...'* (Galatians 5:22–23)

By God's Holy Spirit, a new controlling power of righteousness and purity comes into our lives. This is why Paul wrote,

> *'...be filled with the Spirit, addressing one another in psalms and hymns and spiritual songs, singing and making melody to the Lord, with all your heart, always and for everything giving thanks...'* (Ephesians 5:18–20)

Imagine being around someone whose speech is controlled by the Holy Spirit and always has a thankful heart. They don't grumble or complain, never criticise nor gossip. They aren't negative, and can be relied upon to always tell the truth. They are not sarcastic or flippant and are never argumentative or fault finding. Such a person must be wonderful to know! To be married to someone like that, or be in a church full of people like this must be so refreshing. Remote as the possibility might seem, the responsibility starts with us, to guard against the pollution of our tongue and to seek always to be a blessing in all that we say.

The Psalmist David was very conscious of how far short he came with the problem of his tongue. His desire however, was to be righteous in this area before God, and so he turned to the Lord and asked for help. This was the prayer he expressed and perhaps we too could make it ours,

> *'Let the words of my mouth and meditation of my heart be acceptable in thy sight, O Lord...'* (Psalm 19:14)

Chapter 9

Release from the Burden of Guilt

In the spring of 1959 an Air Force Major was admitted to a Texas Mental Institution. He had been arrested for the crimes of robbery and forgery and had also tried to kill himself twice. His marriage had fallen apart and for a long while he had been drinking heavily. Just a few years earlier, this man had been one of the most promising young officers in the Air Force, heading for a brilliant career. One single, momentous event turned the Major's life upside down. He flew the lead plane over Hiroshima, when the first Atom bomb was dropped.

Shortly afterwards his life changed radically. In his dreams he would see throngs of Japanese men, women and children chasing him. His life began to collapse. The professional psychologists who treated him, said that the Major was subconsciously trying to provoke punishment from society, to atone for the guilt he felt over Hiroshima. Guilt was like a cancer destroying his very soul.

One writer by the name of Bruce Narramore has suggested that guilt in some way is involved in all psychological problems. It has also been described as the place where religion and psychology most often meet. The reasons for a person feeling guilty can be many, and the intensity vary considerably, depending on the individual's sensitivity; their values, perception of other people's reactions and the degree of seriousness of the offence committed.

Some Reasons for Guilt

Firstly – *Violating Personal Standards*
For non-religious and religious alike, both have certain standards and values. It is when these are violated and we act against our own consciences that uncomfortable feelings of regret, remorse and shame come in. Contrary to the view of some theorists like the psychoanalyst Erich Fromm, human nature is not intrinsically and naturally good. The Bible says of us all that,

> *'The heart is deceitful above all things, and desperately corrupt; who can understand it?'* (Jeremiah 17:9)

When we have done, thought, or said something we believe is wrong, or neglected to do something we know should have been done, then we feel a sense of guilt. The Apostle Paul was very aware of this in his own life when he said,

> *'I do not understand my own actions. For I do not do what I want, but I do the very thing I hate.'*
> (Romans 7:15)

At an Anglican Church in St Ives, Cornwall (during a time of prayer and ministry), a lady came forward deeply distressed. With tears of remorse she shared that she had frequently abused her young child and was seeking forgiveness and help to change. Her conscience had been troubling her not just on that Sunday morning, but for a long while prior to that. She was only too aware of her actions being contrary to her own standards.

Sometimes we may act against our better judgement because of pressure put upon us by our peers, to conform and go along with them. Maybe there is pressure from our employers, to 'cut corners' and reach certain production figures and not be completely honest in achieving those aims. In whatever way we contradict our personal values or break standards we, or at times others have set for us, then we feel guilty.

Secondly – *Breaking God's Law*

This is more than violating our own moral code. It is the guilt we feel because God's standard has been broken. In disobeying His word, or in living in a way that is not pleasing to Him, then the conviction of the Holy Spirit makes this known to us. Adam and Eve had no guilt until they broke God's boundaries for them. The moment they did this they felt guilty. This is what Paul meant when he wrote,

> '...through the law comes knowledge of sin.'
>
> (Romans 3:20b)

God's word is like a plumb-line for our life. This came alive to me in a new way several years ago, when I was decorating the bathroom of our house. Having bought all the necessary materials for the job and chosen some tiled wall paper, I started the papering. Taking a quick glance at the walls I decided that they looked reasonably square and as the house was only a few years old it seemed unnecessary to bother with a plumb-line.

You can no doubt guess the rest. As I started to make my way across the wall with the paper, the pattern began sloping off at an angle and it looked awful! If only I'd used the plumb-line this would have given me a 'true' line to start from, and I could have adjusted the paper accordingly. The sloping pattern could easily have been avoided if I had recognised that the wall was not as square as I first thought.

God's word in our lives is just like this, giving us the standard by which we can judge our thoughts, words and actions. It shows us if they do not match God's standard,

151

so that we can alter them and bring them Into line with what is right.

Thirdly – *Failure*

When anyone feels like a failure through yielding to temptation; not being disciplined in prayer and reading the scriptures; or by failing to be a good witness to friends, family and work colleagues, then guilt afflicts their conscience. This can also be the case between husband and wife, when a break down and failure in the relationship comes, maybe ending in divorce, or simply being trapped in a loveless marriage that has drifted apart.

Another common area where failure is experienced is in parenting. What parent hasn't felt guilty when they have wayward teenage children, going through rebellious years? Even though they've done the best they could and there's no cause to be burdened with guilt, still the nagging feeling is there, 'It must be my fault, something I've done or not done must be to blame.' Many fathers also feel guilt because of their failure to spend as much time as they want with their young children. Perhaps a promise has been made to do something special, but then the busyness of work and unexpected pressures have called them away to deal with some immediate problem that has just arisen. The result is they leave disappointed children calling after them, 'But dad – you promised!'

Fourthly – *Unrealistic Expectations*

It is certainly right that we have high standards as Christians and are continually pressing on to be our best for God. In our lives we need goals and objectives to aim for, but these must be realistic. Striving for perfection and never being satisfied with ourselves, to the extent that we always feel we've never quite done enough, can be very unhealthy and lead to a sense of failure and guilt.

Also, trying to please everybody is an unrealistic expectation, which can lead to great bondage. Being fearful of upsetting people, so that we are nervously anxious about doing anything that will cause offence, will bring a continual sense of failure to our lives. If we let our actions be determined by the opinions or criticisms of others then we'll always feel condemned.

An amusing story that illustrates the foolishness of this, tells the tale of an elderly man travelling with a boy and donkey. As they walked through a village, the man was leading and the boy walking behind. The townspeople said the man was a fool for not riding, so to please them he climbed up on the animal's back. When they came to the next village, the people said the old man was cruel to let the child walk while he enjoyed the ride. So, to please them, he got off and set the boy on the animal and continued on his way. In the third village, people accused the child of being lazy for making the old man walk, and the suggestion was made that they both ride. So the man climbed on and they set off again. In the fourth village, the townspeople were indignant at the cruelty to the donkey because he was made to bear the weight of two people. The frustrated man was last seen carrying the donkey down the road!

While this sounds ridiculous, the point is that if we worry about pleasing others we will end up carrying a heavy burden of guilt.

Fifthly – *Uncontrolled Anger*

There is a place for right expressions of anger, against sin and injustice. Where we are aware of ungodliness it needs to be confronted with a righteous response. This strong emotion of righteous indignation motivated the life of Paul to take action against all the idolatry and evil in Athens. The Bible says,

> 'Now while Paul was waiting for them at Athens, his spirit was provoked within him as he saw that the city was full of idols. So he argued in the synagogue with the

*Jews and the devout persons, and in the market place
every day with those who chanced to be there.'*

(Acts 17:16 & 17)

We also see righteous anger in the reaction of Jesus, when
He drove out the money changers who were abusing and
defiling the temple (John 2:13–16).

Anger though, becomes sinful, producing guilt, when it
is uncontrolled, and comes out of a wrong motive or attitude. For example, at times of extreme fatigue an
exhausted mother is at an end of herself and her child
spills milk all over the new carpet; she explodes in a rage
and then feels bad about having done so. Perhaps on occasions when we're made to look foolish in front of others
and because of embarrassment we react to the situation in
anger. Maybe through frustration, having had a difficult
day at work, then finding ourselves bumper to bumper in
long traffic queues on the road. The irritation of this
makes us angry with others. Or maybe as a result of rejection by someone, we feel hurt and offended and there
comes an outburst of harsh words that afterwards we
regret.

It's in these situations that guilt comes into our lives and
is why the Bible says,

'... do not let the sun go down on your anger.'

(Ephesians 4:26b)

Sixthly – *Satan's Attack*

The chief objective of Satan is to bring us into a place of
condemnation and to break our relationship with God.
This is what he did right back in the beginning of creation
and is still doing today. Guilt is one of his main weapons
to attack the child of God. He knows only too well how
this can rob Christians of God's blessings and render them
powerless in service for the Lord. This was the main aim
that Satan had against Job. Knowing that he was considered as *'... a blameless and upright man, who fears God and*

154

turns away from evil' (Job 1:8b), he was set on destroying this relationship. Satan's priority wasn't merely to take Job's riches, possessions, relationships and health. His intention was to bring Job to the place where he would curse God, sin, and be left in a position of guilt.

There are times also when Satan attacks believers to make them feel guilty and unforgiven, even when he has no grounds for doing so. This he achieves with empty accusations, reminding them of past sins that have already been confessed and forgiven by the Lord. The Bible speaks about him as,

> *'... the accuser of our brethren ... who accuses them day and night before our God.'*   (Revelation 12:10b)

These taunts ought to have no effect because the past has been dealt with. However, if Satan can cause an individual to focus on past sins, then a feeling of guilt and condemnation will creep in again. By whispering lies and sowing doubts there develops the torment of uncertainty regarding God's forgiveness.

One young man from Telford had this problem. Every time I went to preach there, he would come up to me after the meeting, troubled about committing the 'unforgivable sin'. Each time we talked and prayed together but he remained in bondage to guilt, preoccupied with this thought. There was a definite satanic attack upon his life, and no reason for him to be tormented by such thinking, but he would believe the lies whispered to him by the enemy more than the truth of God's word.

The Result of Guilt

Guilt in itself is not always a negative thing, because the prompting we feel in our conscience, can stimulate us to change our behaviour where necessary. However there is no doubt that guilt can have harmful, inhibiting influences that make life miserable.

Firstly – *Disillusionment and Despair*

Regardless of how important people might think they are in their own eyes, or how highly they are regarded by others, when faced with eternity their perspectives change. If they've lived independently of God then guilt can leave them feeling helpless and hopeless, and their life's work meaningless.

This was very much the case with the influential author and founder member of the Fabian Society, H.G. Wells. As he looked back on his life just before he died, he wrote these words,

> 'The science to which I pinned my faith is bankrupt. Its counsels which should have established the millennium led instead directly to the suicide of Europe. I believed them once. In their name I helped destroy the faith of millions of worshippers in the temples of a thousand creeds. And now they look at me and witness the great tragedy of an atheist who has lost his faith.'

Nobody knows whether we are at the beginning, middle or end of our lives. One thing is sure though, when we live contrary to God's Word, this sin will eventually lead to guilt, which if we do nothing about, will ultimately result in disillusionment and despair.

Secondly – *Physical Conflict*

In previous chapters I have mentioned that sickness can be caused by such things as anxiety, resentment, and an absence of the fear of God. When we consider also the area of guilt, this too can produce illness if it is left unresolved. The fact that unconfessed sin can have a very definite effect upon our bodies is seen in the experience of King David. Because he tried to suppress his guilt and hide his sin he became sick not just spiritually but physically. This we see as he writes,

'When I declared not my sin, my body wasted away through my groaning all day long. For day and night thy hand was heavy upon me; my strength was dried up as by the heat of summer. I acknowledged my sin to thee, and I did not hide my iniquity; I said, "I will confess my transgressions to the Lord;" then thou didst forgive the guilt of my sin.' (Psalm 32:3–5)

Whenever tension builds in a person and is not released, the body weakens and eventually breaks down. Several years ago, a highly respected psychologist (who made no claim to be a Christian), by the name of O. Hobart Mowrer, wrote about this conflict in his book *The Crisis in Psychology and Religion*. He said,

'Man sickens in mind, soul and body because of unconfessed and unatoned guilt. Mental illness is really moral illness that can only be cured by confession to significant other people and by the making of restitution.'

The Apostle Paul also gives us an insight to the effect of unconfessed sin damaging a person's health. Writing to the Church at Corinth he said,

'Whoever, therefore, eats the bread or drinks the cup of the Lord in an unworthy manner will be guilty of profaning the body and blood of the Lord. Let a man examine himself, and so eat of the bread and drink of the cup. For any one who eats and drinks without discerning the body eats and drinks judgement upon himself. **That is why many of you are weak and ill, and some have died.'** (1 Corinthians 11:27–30)

Thirdly – *Self-Condemnation*

The presence of guilt in a person's life has the affect of making that individual uncomfortable about themselves. Sometimes though, the impact can be far greater, causing them to feel worthless and dirty, even beyond the love of God.

While preaching at Gravesend in Kent, I met a lady in this condition. She was an elderly woman who worked on the fish market. As we sat talking together her hardened, wrinkled face showed the evidence of many years spent away from the Lord. She said, 'I want so much to believe, but God could never forgive me for the things I've done in my life!' We talked at length, and as I explained the grace of God more clearly, a light started to dawn upon her dark solemn expression. I read the words of Paul to her which said,

> *'There is therefore now no condemnation for those who are in Christ Jesus.'* (Romans 8:1)

A short time later she said she wanted to put her trust in Christ and become a Christian. At this point her whole face just lit up and she looked a completely changed woman! She had stopped condemning herself, because she could see that God did not condemn her.

Self-condemnation can become so debilitating for people that in certain situations it can be taken to the extreme of self-hatred, resulting in self-inflicted punishment on their bodies. This is the case sometimes with those who have been sexually abused, or people suffering from eating disorders such as anorexia and bulimia. The guilt that they feel is often in no way appropriate. They may be innocent of any wrong relating to the initial, underlying cause of the problem. However, there is still guilt tormenting them, because in some way they blame themselves for their circumstances and hate themselves because of this.

Fourthly – *Self-Justification*
Here is the opposite extreme to what we have just mentioned, but still one of the results of guilt. This is a

desperate attempt to cover up guilt feelings through rationalising and excusing sin.

Recently, I was talking to a leader of a fellowship in the Midlands after speaking at his church. He was married, with children, but found himself attracted to one of his church members. Frequent visits to the woman's home had been made and he said to me, 'We've not actually "done" anything, but I have kissed her.' He wanted to continue seeing this person just as a 'friend', and for the relationship to go no further than that. All his comments as we spoke were trying to justify his position and their continued 'friendship'. I said to him, that in his heart he already knew the only answer was to immediately sever the relationship and no longer go round to her house alone. While conceding that this was the right thing to do, at the same time he was still making excuses why this couldn't be done.

Another form of self-justification is trying to appease the conscience through good works. Here a person feels the need to justify their worth and earn God's approval. They are uncertain that they've been 'productive enough' to deserve God's blessing. Guilt feelings are some of the reasons we both punish and push ourselves to keep doing better.

This was the torment that Martin Luther, one of the early church reformers, battled with for many years. Born on November 10th 1483 into a devout Catholic family, he grew up to become a monk, living a pious life, according to strict rules and observances. Because of a particularly sensitive conscience he was always greatly troubled by guilt feelings and could never be sure he had confessed everything, or had not committed some new sin. Writing about this he said,

> 'The more I tried to remedy an uncertain and afflicted conscience with the traditions of men, the more each day I found it more uncertain, weaker and more trouble.'

This state of nervous tension, trying through good works to rid himself of guilt, continued relentlessly. Then one day a verse from the Bible broke into the darkness of his understanding,

> *'He who through faith is righteous shall live.'*
>
> (Romans 1:17b)

This resulted in him being set free from striving and he came to a place of faith in God's grace of forgiveness through Christ alone.

The Remedy to Guilt

The Bible gives us some very clear and definite steps to remedy this problem of guilt. Through the gospel of Jesus Christ this curse upon mankind can be broken and a lasting, life-changing peace experienced.

Firstly – *Genuine Repentance*

This is not just a desire to avoid the consequences of wrong actions, or a regret simply that we've been found out. Repentance is initially an inward change coming from genuine sorrow that we have sinned against God.

Take the example of a burglar, who having broken into a jewellery shop has filled his pockets full of all that he can lay his hands on. He runs out of the shop right into the arms of the law. The policeman cautions him with the words, 'You do not have to say anything, but what you do say may be taken down and used in evidence against you.' The burglar then might respond, 'Well, I'm very sorry for what I've done, and it'll never happen again.' Obviously his sorrow is not genuine repentance, he's just sorry that he didn't get away with it! This is what Paul refers to when he says,

> *'For godly grief produces a repentance that leads to salvation and brings no regret, but worldly grief produces death.'* (2 Corinthians 7:10)

160

Genuine repentance comes through the Holy Spirit's conviction as we are reminded what our sin did to Jesus and it will always result in a changed life.

Billy Graham was once preaching on repentance and having proclaimed this uncompromisingly, a man came up to him after the meeting, white with rage. Greatly agitated he said, 'Do you realise with that sort of preaching on repentance, you must have put the Church back at least 200 years!' The reply from Billy Graham was immediate. In his polite, respectful way he apologised to the angry man. 'I'm very sorry,' he said, 'I certainly did not intend to put the church back 200 years, I intended to put the Church back 2,000 years!'

What he was saying was that the gospel we need to return to, which lays the axe to the root of all our problems, is repentance. This was the first message Jesus began his ministry with that we read of in Mark 1:15. He said,

> 'The time is fulfilled, and the Kingdom of God is at hand; repent, and believe the gospel.'

The word 'repent' means 'a change of mind', literally a 'turning about'. It results in a change of direction, a change of attitude and a change of action.

Secondly – *Faith in the Blood of Christ*
The Bible says,

> '... the blood of Jesus Christ his Son cleanses us from all sin.'   (1 John 1:7b)

Several years ago we had a door to door salesman call on us selling a new type of vacuum cleaner. It was extremely expensive, costing several hundred pounds, but it was guaranteed to clean far more thoroughly than any other cleaner on the market. As part of his demonstration he asked us to get our own vacuum out and vigorously run it over a patch of carpet until we were satisfied it was clean.

161

When this was done he proceeded to use his vacuum over the same area. As his equipment was for demonstration purposes, it had a white filter and clear glass fitted in such a way that you could see what was being picked up.

When we examined the white filter it was full of dirt which had been picked up from the area that we had considered clean. Noticing that he had suitably impressed us, he continued to carry out the same test on our furniture and curtains with similar results. Then we went to the bedroom and were asked to thoroughly vacuum the mattress on our bed. He then proceeded to do the same with his cleaner and the outcome was astonishing. The white filter was full of a flaky grey substance. 'What do you think that is,' he said with a certain air of confidence. When we told him we didn't know he replied, 'Skin! Dead skin, that's what it is!'

We were so sure that we had cleaned everything. Yet all around us, in spite of our hard work, there was dirt that we couldn't remove from our carpets, settee, curtains and even our bed! In thinking of this I'm reminded that our best efforts can never make our life clean before a holy God. Only the wonderful power of the blood of Jesus can rid us of sin and deal absolutely with the dirt of a guilty conscience.

The Bible says,

> 'If we confess our sins, he is faithful and just, and will forgive our sins and cleanse us from all unrighteousness.' (1 John 1:9)

As we come in confession, and put our faith in Christ's blood which was shed that we might be forgiven, we can know a life that is 100% clean from sin. Then like Christian in John Bunyan's *Pilgrim's Progress*, we feel a great burden of guilt roll off our shoulders.

Thirdly – Receive the Grace of Restoration
Because God forgives and accepts us we must receive that

grace and stop looking back to the mistakes and sins of our past. The words of Jesus to the woman who had been caught in the act of adultery reveals the heart of God's grace. She had been dragged before Jesus by people who insisted the law required she should be stoned to death because of her sin. His response was,

> '... Let him who is without sin among you be the first to throw a stone at her.' (John 8:7b)

One by one they all slipped away because they were all sinners, and she was left alone, feeling guilty and unclean in the presence of the spotless Son of God. Jesus then asked her,

> 'Woman, where are they? Has no one condemned you?' She replied, 'No one, Lord.' (John 8:10 & 11a)

Then came those wonderful words of grace, setting the woman free and giving her back her dignity. Jesus said,

> '... Neither do I condemn you; go, and do not sin again.' (John 8:11b)

The Lord wants people not only to be released from guilt but also to be fully restored in their relationship with Him. Just like the prodigal son in Luke 15. When there is an acknowledgement of sin and genuine repentance, there is no condemnation. Regardless of how far a person has backslidden and no matter what a person has done, God's heart reaches out to accept and restore the repentant sinner.

To illustrate more fully this grace of love and restoration, a man by the name of Max Lucado tells the true story of Maria and her teenage daughter Christina, who lived in Brazil. The young girl was tired of life in her dusty village and longed for the excitement of the big city. One morning her mother found Christina's bed empty. Maria knew straight away where her daughter had gone. She also knew immediately what she must do to find her. Quickly throwing some clothes in a bag, she gathered up all her money, and ran out of the house. On her way to the bus stop she entered a drug store to get one last thing, pictures. She sat in the photo booth, closed the curtains, and spent all she could on pictures of herself. With her purse full of small black and white photos she boarded the next bus to Rio de Janeiro.

Maria knew Christina had no way of earning money and also that her daughter was too stubborn to give up. When pride meets hunger a person will do things that were before unthinkable. With this in mind Maria began her search. Bars, hotels, night clubs; any place with the reputation for street walkers and prostitutes. She went to them all and at each place she left a picture; taped on a bathroom mirror, tacked onto a hotel bulletin board, fastened to a corner phone booth. It wasn't long before both the money and pictures ran out, and Maria had to go home. The weary mother wept as the bus began its long journey back to her small village.

A few weeks later Christina descended the stairs of a seedy hotel. Her young face was tired. Her brown eyes no longer danced with youth, but spoke of pain and fear. Her laughter was broken and her dream had become a nightmare. A thousand times over she had longed to trade the countless beds for the secure home she had left. Yet the village was, in too many ways, too far away. As she reached the bottom of the stairs, her eyes noticed a familiar face. She looked again, and there on the lobby mirror was a small picture of her mother. Christina's eyes burned and her throat tightened as she walked across the room and removed the small photo. Written on the back was this compelling invitation, 'Whatever you have done, whatever you have become, it doesn't matter, I love you, please come home.'

Fourthly – *Keep Alert to the Dangers of Falling*

It is often when we least expect it and are caught off guard, that we are in the most danger. The Bible warns us against this complacency when it says,

> *'Therefore let any one who thinks that he stands take heed lest he fall.'*   (1 Corinthians 10:12)

In July 1911, a stuntman named Bobby Leach went over Niagara Falls in a specially designed steel drum and lived to tell the tale. Although he suffered minor injuries, he survived because he recognised the tremendous dangers involved in the feat, and because he had done everything he could to protect himself from harm. Several years later, while walking down a street in New Zealand, he slipped on some orange peel, fell, and badly fractured his leg. He was taken to hospital where he later died because of complications.

Bobby Leach received greater injury walking down the street, than in going over Niagara Falls, simply because he was not prepared for danger, in what he assumed to be a safe place. We must always be alert and watchful because the enemy of our souls will try to cause us to fall. It is essential not only to recognise the danger of temptation, but also take every precaution to protect ourselves from harm. The best way to do this is:

(a) Reverencing God's Word – The scriptures can bring us great safety, but only when we esteem them highly. This is exactly the attitude of the psalmist when he says in Psalm 119:9–11,

> *'How can a young man keep his way pure? By guarding it according to thy word. With my whole heart I seek thee; let me not wander from thy commandments! I*

have laid up thy word in my heart, that I might not sin against thee.'

(b) Resisting Temptation – We need to see temptation not as sin, merely an invitation to sin. There is a choice involved, we do not have to accept the invitation. In Galatians 5:1 it says,

> *'For freedom Christ has set us free; stand fast therefore, and do not submit again to a yoke of slavery.'*

We have a responsibility to stand firm against temptation, if we don't, then we come under a yoke of bondage again.

(c) Renewal in the Holy Spirit – As we mentioned in the previous chapter the ability to overcome and walk in victory can never be achieved in our own strength. To be able to counter spiritual attack, we need to live Spirit-filled lives. This is why the power of the Holy Spirit is so relevant in our battle against temptation. God's word says,

> *'Live by the Spirit, and you will not gratify the desires of the sinful nature.'*   (Galatians 5:16, NIV)

Fifthly – *Commitment to Godliness*
With Jesus we see that while His grace and forgiveness continually reaches out to restore those who feel guilty and condemned, He never relaxes His standards. To the adulterous woman Jesus said, *'. . . go and do not sin again'* (John 8:11b). We are freed from our guilt that we might live for the glory of God. The only way we can do this is by committing ourselves to developing a godly life. It is an inescapable fact that **the Blood claims all those that it cleanses**. This is why the Bible says,

> *'. . . You are not your own; you were bought with a price. So glorify God in your body.'*
> (1 Corinthians 6:19–20)

166

We cannot live how we please; our lives are to be kept pure and righteous because we belong to God. The only way of remaining free from guilt is by yielding ourselves completely to the Lord and taking responsibility to get rid of everything that is an offence to Him. God will not do it all, we have to maintain this freedom.

Just a few months ago while preaching in Birmingham, a man came after the meeting to tell me that the last time I was speaking at his church he responded for prayer. He said, 'Just after you prayed my car was stolen on two occasions!' Surprised by his bright positive face I said, 'Well why are you so pleased?' He replied, 'When my car was returned, the only thing that was stolen from it was some pornographic magazines. I'd been struggling to get rid of them for a long time!' While he saw this as God's intervention in his life, I don't believe the Lord will get people out of such situations if the heart of the problem is not dealt with. The temptation can be removed, but something still needs to be done about the root cause of unrighteousness.

In the same way that sinful habits are formed through regular practice, we can also develop righteous habits too. If we are to know victory over guilt, then we must train ourselves in godliness (1 Timothy 4:7b). When a Christian directs his life towards this goal, through discipline, the practice of godliness becomes 'natural'. As we practice what God tells us to do, holiness will become part of us. Taking responsibility in this way enables us to break out of the vicious circle of sinning, confession, and sinning again. We can then know a life free from the burden of guilt.

Chapter 10

Finding Hope in Depression

It was a day of great excitement for us as a family, when we moved from our terraced house in Exeter, to a new estate some five miles away. I was nearly nine years of age, and with wide eyes I looked through the window at the new horizons that lay before me. Deciding to go out and explore what seemed like another world, I put on my little bobble hat, wellington boots and duffle coat. Then with much enthusiasm, I set off, walking across the boggy fields beyond the building site nearby. I didn't get very far before I found myself stuck in an area of mud and unable to move. The more I struggled the deeper I sank, until eventually the cold, slimy mud came up over the top of my boots and squelched down inside to my feet. With the vivid imagination of a child, and having seen many cowboy films of people falling into quick-sand, never to be seen again, I 'knew' the same thing was going to happen to me!

In panic, my immediate reaction was to shout at the top of my voice, crying for help. At the ear-piercing sound of my screams, one of the workmen from the nearby building site came rushing along. Seeing my predicament, he lifted me up (leaving my little wellington boots in the mud!), and carried me across to the more secure ground of the road-side. It felt such a relief to be rescued from what seemed like a terrifying situation, where I was completely helpless.

This incident, though thirty years ago, has always stayed in my mind, particularly now as we come to this chapter on depression. It reminds me of what the Psalmist felt as he spoke of the Lord's deliverance in his life. He said,

> '*I waited patiently for the Lord; he inclined to me and heard my cry. He drew me up from the desolate pit, out of the miry bog, and set my feet upon a rock, making my steps secure. He put a new song in my mouth, a song of praise to our God...* '　　　　(Psalm 40:1–3)

This is the good news for every person struggling with depression. God in His mercy and love is able to lift people out of the pit of their despair. He can set them on a solid foundation and give them a song of joy once again to sing.

Someone I spoke to recently who experienced this, was a leader I met while preaching at a church in Suffolk. He had been suffering with severe depression for many months and according to his wife was also suicidal. Through the ministry that evening God brought deliverance to his life. The following morning as we talked at the breakfast table, he said that a breakthrough had come in his depression and he felt better than he had done for a long time!

What is Depression?

It is a very complex and widespread problem all too common among Christians as well as non-believers. For many it is truly like a 'desolate pit' or 'miry bog' where there is no sound of joy. The more people try to struggle out, the deeper they feel themselves going under. Known as the 'common cold of mental disorders', it can occur at any age and has been recognised as a problem for more than two thousand years. The Greek physician Hippocrates of Cos, described it four hundred years before Christ. Today with all the many pressures of modern life it has come much more into prominence. An article in the Journal of the American Medical Association, written by N. Kline says,

'More human suffering has resulted from depression than from any other single disease afflicting mankind.'

Depressive Syndromes can be viewed as a kind of spectrum with sadness at one end of the scale and severe psychosis (extreme mental illness involving the whole personality) at the other. We all get depressed at times in the rough and tumble of life, but for many people, depression is a real and ever present problem, and for them it can become a living nightmare.

For some the experience of low moods is no more than a fleeting moment, or something they can dispel. But for others it is much more severe and disabling and lasts a great deal longer. The experience is like a dark prison that is terrifying and impenetrable. For no apparent reason a person can feel unbearably sad, their world turns grey and it seems impossible to talk themselves out of what is descending upon them. In this condition the worst thing in the world is to have an insensitive individual trying to 'buck them up', by saying, 'Snap out of it,' or 'Pull yourself together!' This approach almost always will have the reverse effect upon the depressed person.

While the spectrum of what we are talking about is wide, it is important to underline the distinction between severe depression and unhappiness. When someone is unhappy they are still able to seek help and be comforted by others to ease the pain. In severe depression however, it seems as though neither the sympathy nor concern of others can get through the wall that separates them from those trying to help.

As we consider this problem, there are four important things the person needs to realise right from the start, that can begin to bring hope into what seems an impossible situation.

Firstly – *They are Not Alone*
Many others feel just as they do now. In fact according to the World Health Organisation, more than 100 million people in the world are depressed at any one time. Those who are suffering like this are often amazed to discover that there are others, including Christians, who feel exactly like they do. It can be a relief to realise that they are not the only ones experiencing what seems like madness. One of our country's finest preachers was C.H. Spurgeon who lived from 1834–1892. Frequently during his ministry he was plunged into deep depression. In his autobiography entitled *The Full Harvest*, he says,

> 'During the time that I have been preaching the gospel in this place I have suffered many times of severe sickness and frightful mental depression, sinking almost to despair.'

Secondly – *They are Not Failures*
This is exactly what depressed people think they are. Because of their problem they feel in some way, 'useless' and 'no good'. However, some of the greatest names that have lived and who accomplished the most outstanding things have been depressives. Their names include such people as Composers, Beethoven, and Robert Schumann; Poet, William Cowper; Scientist, Sir Isaac Newton; Writer and Philosopher, Leo Tolstoy; Statesman and Prime Minister, Sir Winston Churchill; and two of the funniest Comedians in the world of entertainment, Tony Hancock and Spike Milligan. This is not mentioned to encourage a complacent attitude about the condition of depression, thus accepting it; the point is made to dispel any feeling of defeatism and to stimulate confidence. Each individual has tremendous potential, even when that ability lies dormant beneath the cloud of depression.

Thirdly – *The very Worst Times do Pass*

Although the battle might feel hopeless and the darkness endless, there is real hope for every person struggling with depression. What seems like an immovable, insurmountable barrier of gloom can be overcome, not only now, but for good. The end may appear nowhere in sight, but victory and freedom is not far away. This is why the Psalmist says,

> '... *Weeping may tarry for the night, but joy comes with the morning.*' (Psalm 30:5b)

Just as the darkest night is broken by the dawning of a new day, the long, lonely experience of how they feel will give way to brighter times.

This was so for a lady who came to me after a Baptism service in Lancashire at which I was speaking. Her testimony was that seven months before, when I was last at the Church, she asked for prayer. For over a year she had been suffering with depression, but after ministry that night she said the depression went, and the Lord had completely set her free!

Fourthly –
Broken Fellowship with God Must be Restored

Depression will break a person's fellowship with God, if they allow their feelings to govern their faith, and feelings are the dominating factor with depressed people. Temporary help can be experienced in medication and from 'specialists', but ultimately the answer is found through faith in God. They need to come to the place where they are willing to do exactly what His word says, even when they don't feel like it.

A young Christian man called Jim Elliot lived and died by this principle. He was one of four missionaries who were murdered deep in Ecuador's rain forests, in January 1956. Their killers were savage Auca Indians, the very people they had been seeking to reach for Christ. Though their mission was full of danger and hardship they remained faithful, strengthened by their relationship with God. Throughout his Christian service Jim Elliot was determined to overcome every negative feeling that would try to hinder his fellowship with God. He said,

> 'If godliness is to be a state of soul within me, I will no longer depend on pleasant impulses to bring me before the Lord. I must rather respond to principles I know to be right, whether I feel them to be enjoyable or not.'

Warning Signs

By being alert and sensitive to the early warning signs in a depressed person, the condition can be prevented from developing into something more serious and prolonged. One of the greatest regrets in my own life was not recognising these symptoms sooner, when my wife had a period of depression several years ago. As I look back now, I know if I'd been more aware of them, greater support and understanding could have been given, which would have made a big difference to her recovery.

Sometimes these symptoms can be masked by a brave face that the person presents to the outside world. A well known story that illustrates this is told of a man with deep depression visiting the doctor. No advice or medication seemed to relieve the person of the intense despair and sadness he felt. Eventually, as a last resort, the doctor suggested that his patient went along to the circus that regularly came to town. There he said was a famous clown who was well known for making even the most desolate person laugh. At this suggestion the man slowly looked up and with a sad, helpless expression responded, 'Doctor, I am that clown!'

Though the depressed person may hide behind a mask

of pretence, the warning signs will be there, and these changes in behaviour can easily be noticed. They are:

(a) Loss of energy – A continual sense of fatigue is evident and the body feels physically heavy and burdensome. Even when depressives get up in the morning they are not refreshed but feel tired and each little job is an effort. Minor chores become a major task and the person's movements get slower, causing it to take longer to complete daily responsibilities. The time drags so that every minute seems like an hour. They lose their appetite both for life and food, and this lack of food intake also contributes to their lack of energy. Difficulty in sleeping is common, again adding to the overall feeling of tiredness. They will often find themselves waking up in early hours of the morning, just lying there brooding, dreading the approach of another day.

(b) Loss of interest – Because it becomes hard for the depressed person to get motivated, simply getting out of a chair, or bed in the morning seems pointless. Depressed people feel as though they just don't want to bother. Their interest in work, hobbies, conversation and sex wanes as their spirits dwindle, and so withdrawal becomes their escape. This is accompanied by a loss of interest in making decisions and planning ahead. Feeling little or no purpose to their lives causes a lack of spontaneity and ability to enjoy what previously had been pleasurable activities. In this state of severe depression, their loss of interest would extend to the extreme of contemplating suicide, because to them, life is no longer worth living.

(c) Self-Criticism – The feeling of being unable to cope makes depressed people very hard on themselves, and a great deal of self-blame and shame develops. Household chores get neglected, and responsibilities pile up, which only compounds their feelings of inadequacy and helplessness. Letting themselves go in appearance and losing pride in themselves adds to their negative feelings of worthlessness. The attitude of self-criticism causes the person to be ultra-sensitive and so each mistake or problem gets exaggerated. They continually make mountains out of mole-hills, which results in a constant state of high anxiety.

(d) Moodiness – There is an ever present sense of gloom, sadness, crying, loss of affection and humour, so that to smile at anything feels impossible. Utter loneliness and intense despair is felt where it seems as though no one understands. Irritability and intolerance of others is common and their thoughts are preoccupied with being victims of someone else's actions or their own circumstances. Such people are only able to focus on themselves, dwelling just on their problems and feelings. In doing so they completely forget about the needs of others. This results in them becoming extremely selfish and self-centred, and very difficult to live with.

Causes for Depression

Physical Factors
It is important when trying to understand depression, not to immediately jump to the conclusion that the problem must be 'spiritual'. It may well be, but there are other causes. We need to consider the physical state of the person to begin with. A healthy body is less susceptible to both mental and physical illnesses. For this reason the family doctor should be contacted straight away when there are any prolonged changes in mood-swings or behaviour. This is not so they can be instantly put on anti-depressants, but that skilled, professional and practical help may be given. Simply being able to talk to such a person brings reassurance to victims of depression. This enables them to see things in perspective and then appropriate help can also be prescribed.

The person could be suffering from general 'burn out' through overwork, or possibly a chemical imbalance in the body. Perhaps deficiencies in certain essential items of diet, especially members of the vitamin B and C group might be making them feel under the weather and miserable. Food allergies and peculiar reactions to particular medicines, food colourings and additives may induce depression with some. Also (strange as it may sound), a cause of depression with certain susceptible people, is a lack of sufficient natural light in the winter. This condition is known under the rather appropriately named acronym of SAD – 'Seasonal Affected Disorder'.

The mother having just had her new baby might be depressed because of an imbalance of hormones, lack of sleep and general exhaustion. Also following a viral infection and illness such as influenza, hepatitis, or glandular fever, a person might not have fully recovered and still be weak physically and emotionally. Low spirits can linger months after such physical problems.

Negative Thinking

Some by their very disposition may be more prone to depression than others. These people tend to see the dark side of life and overlook the positive. They are more negative by nature and life seems a succession of burdens, obstacles and defeats. They usually have a negative view of themselves and feel deficient, inadequate, and incapable of performing efficiently. The future is also viewed in a negative way so that as they look ahead they see only hardships, frustrations and hopelessness.

This attitude of pessimism lowers the expectation for anything good to happen to them. It is the sort of thinking that if a light can be seen at the end of the tunnel, then it must be the light of an oncoming train! Or the outlook of the woman who said, 'I always feel the worst when I feel the best, because I know how bad I'm going to feel when I start to feel worse again!'

Life's Stresses

This is a major factor leading to depression. If physically our strength is low, our emotions fragile and in our thinking life seems dark, then when the inevitable knocks of circumstances occur it all becomes too much. Depression is often rooted in some kind of underlying anxiety or emotional difficulty. This might be the stress of an adverse environment at work, or maybe being out of work for any length of time and feeling a loss of self-esteem. The feeling of loss in a whole variety of things can affect people in quite dramatic ways. For instance, loss of opportunity, job, status, freedom, possessions, health etc. Also the loss of relations through death, divorce or prolonged separation can trigger off a feeling of stress that leads to depression.

Suppressed Anger

The result of 'bottling up' emotions of anger is resentment, which is often at the root of depression. One psychologist by the name of Roger Barrett describes it in saying,

'Resentment is the accumulation of unexpressed anger, and is the most destructive emotion in human relationships and in personal well being. Some depressed people wallow in depression as a means of hurting others, as if the depression itself becomes an indirect expression of hostility.

It's almost as if they were saying, "I am depressed and there's nothing you can do about it. It's all your fault and if you don't give me attention and sympathy, I may get even more depressed or do something desperate." It's a kind of psychological blackmail. Suicide attempts (which most often occur in depressed people) not infrequently have this characteristic. There's a kind of, "See what you made me do" or, "Now you will miss me" quality to the notes or communications surrounding the tragedy. They blame others for their bad feelings.'

Unresolved Guilt

This is probably one of the biggest causes of depression today and as we saw from the last chapter, something we all have to deal with. Failure to handle responsibilities or problems in God's way, triggers our consciences and bad feelings result. If these are not heeded, they can lead to depression. This is acutely felt by people who are led to believe, 'Christians should never have difficulties with depression.' Most churches know so little about this particular problem, that the individual who becomes trapped in such a pit, is left feeling condemned and isolated.

We may feel guilty about various sins, but sexual immorality is one that causes depression, even years after the sin has been committed. All sexual activity outside a marriage relationship will cause guilt, and can eventually lead to depression. A friend of mine, who has been in fulltime ministry for over twenty five years, speaks of how this underlies some cases of depression. He mentions one married couple he knew that had been involved in a 'wife swapping' weekend. The wife was reluctant to go along with this, but persuaded by her husband, eventually gave way to his pressure. Many years later, she began suffering with severe depression and was admitted to a psychiatric hospital. The cause of her problem was identified as unresolved guilt, which she felt over the immoral activities she had been drawn into.

The Answer to Depression

I mentioned earlier that the cause of depression is not always spiritual, but having said this, in most cases there will be a spiritual problem involved in how it has been handled. By our attitudes and reactions to the problem we can create or feed depression ourselves. The wise, ancient Greek philosopher, Epictatus said,

> 'It is not things in themselves which trouble us, but the opinions we have about these things.'

In the same way, it is not pressure or problems that affect us but our response towards them. To change our feelings we must first change the response of our thinking. Freedom comes as we reach out to the Lord by faith and respond to scriptural principles, in spite of how we feel. Psalm 121 gives four steps that help us to do this.

Firstly – *Look Beyond Self and Circumstances*

Some people, because of the burden they feel in depression, actually appear physically bowed down. Finding hope is possible as we begin to look up, not merely physically but in our faith saying,

> *'But thou, O Lord, art a shield about me, my glory, and the lifter of my head.'* (Psalm 3:3)

The first important step that must be taken is to **choose** to stop being self-centred, and look beyond the immediate darkness. This is what we find in Psalm 121:1. The Psalmist says,

> *'I lift up my eyes to the hills. From whence comes my help?'*

What is needed is a positive decision, a step taken as an act of the will to seek for an answer outside of ourselves and other people. This then makes room for God to come into the situation.

No matter how grim our circumstances, and in spite of how we might feel, we really do have the ability by God's grace, to look further than what is confronting us. The Apostle Paul went through many difficult experiences yet he could say,

> *'... we look not to the things that are seen but to the things that are unseen; for the things that are seen are transient, but the things that are unseen are eternal.'* (2 Corinthians 4:18)

The key principle that governed his life was to lift up his eyes and look beyond himself and his circumstances. This was put very much to the test when Paul and Silas had been viciously beaten, thrown into a dark prison and their feet fastened in stocks. Even in such a dire situation we read,

> *'But about midnight Paul and Silas were praying and singing hymns to God, and the prisoners were listening to them.'* (Acts 16:25)

This same principle is seen even more clearly in the Old Testament when Elisha and his servant were together at a city called Dothan. The king of Syria had sent a large army to capture them and during the night they surrounded the place where the two were staying. When the servant got up the next morning, he looked out of the window and was filled with fear by what he saw. Running to wake Elisha, he cried out anxiously, wanting to know what to do. The response from the prophet in this life and death situation was remarkable. The Bible says he calmly replied,

> *'Fear not, for those who are with us are more than those who are with them.'* (2 Kings 6:16)

Then Elisha looked up and said,

> *'O Lord, I pray thee, open his eyes that he may see.'* (2 Kings 6:17a)

At that very moment the servant's eyes were opened, and then he could see the great host of the armies of heaven, encompassed around the enemy. They were there all the time but only Elisha could see them!

The servant was full of gloom because all he was looking at was his immediate problem. Elisha on the other hand found hope in difficulty, because he was looking past what he could see with his natural sight. He chose to lift up his eyes and see beyond himself and his circumstances. The great need with all depressive people is to start doing the same and to break out of their self-centredness. Nobody would suggest that it's easy, but it is certainly possible.

Secondly –
Let your Mind Focus on the Greatness of God
Having taken that initial step of looking beyond self, it is now essential to focus on God. For those who are struggling with depression their revelation of God will be blurred and distorted by how they feel and what they've been thinking. In Psalm 121:2 we find this next step. The Psalmist says,

> '*My help comes from the Lord, **who made heaven and earth**.*'

It is in recognising who God is, and what He is able to do, that hope is strengthened. One of the great secrets of living in victory is – **Look at your problem through God and don't try to look at God through your problem**. If we get this the wrong way round, then all that we see is a giant of a problem and a very small God. But when we are looking at our problem focused on God first, we see His glory, His majesty, His faithfulness and His power. Our problem is then brought into perspective, as we see it for the true size that it is.

Years ago, whenever I felt emotionally low and needed to see things in proportion, I would go to one of the large parks in Exeter late at night, seeking God's direction. In walking through the darkness with nobody else around, I would just lift up my eyes and begin to think of the greatness of the God who created the wonder of all that I could see. As I did this, a tremendous verse of an old hymn would come flooding to mind. Its words translated into English by Stuart K. Hine are:

'**Oh Lord my God!** when I in awesome wonder
Consider all the works Thy hand has made,
I see the stars, I hear the mighty thunder,
Thy power throughout the Universe displayed:
Then sings my soul, my Saviour God to Thee,
How great Thou art! How great Thou art!'

It was this continual discovery and fresh revelation of
the majesty of God, that helped me to see my problems in
their true light. One of the best passages of scripture that
enables us to focus on God's greatness was written by the
prophet Isaiah. He said,

> *'For to us a child is born, to us a son is given; and the
> government will be upon his shoulder, and his name will
> be called "Wonderful Counsellor, Mighty God, Ever-
> lasting Father, Prince of Peace."'* (Isaiah 9:6)

Focusing upon God as the, *'Wonderful Counsellor'*,
directs us to the truth that He alone has the answer to our
problem. Seeing Him as the *'Mighty God'*, reminds us that
He is not someone merely of talk, but of supernatural ability. It is His miraculous power that is able to change what
seems to be unchangeable. In dwelling upon His nature as
the *'Everlasting Father'*, we are encouraged that He hasn't
just got an answer to our problem, nor merely power to
bring the miracle we need. As our Father He has the concern, and the willingness to respond to our cry. Then when
we see God as the *'Prince of Peace'*, we're reassured that
the one who was able to still the raging storm with just a
word of command, is also able to bring peace to the storms
in our emotions and thoughts.

Thirdly – *Listen and Believe the Promises of God*
This next step is a natural progression from the previous
two. Having looked beyond self and circumstances, then
focused on the greatness of God, we now need to listen

carefully and have faith in what He has to say. The promises of God are just like a vitamin pill; all the goodness of God condensed into one short sentence! These promises express His care and protection towards us, especially in difficult times. It is by feeding on them that we regain our health and strength.

In Psalm 121, we have eight wonderful promises. It's as we believe them with all our hearts that we give God the opportunity to honour His word in our life. These promises are found from verses 3–8. Here the Bible tells us:

(1) *'He will not let your foot be moved.'*
(2) *'He who keeps you will not slumber.'*
(3) *'The Lord is your keeper.'*
(4) *'The Lord is your shade on your right hand.'*
(5) *'The sun shall not smite you by day, nor the moon by night.'*
(6) *'The Lord will keep you from all evil.'*
(7) *'He will keep your life.'*
(8) *'The Lord will keep your going out and your coming in from this time forth and forever more.'*

One young man during World War II was particularly grateful for these promises. He was a naval pilot making an air strike against the Japanese-held Chichi Jima island. His plane was struck by anti-aircraft fire, and he had to bail out over the Pacific. Another pilot spotted his chute just as it hit the water and radioed his position. Within minutes, the submarine USS Finback surfaced and rescued the flyer. Safely on board, he silently thanked God for sparing his life. That young pilot was George Bush who became America's 41st President.

It is by listening to God's Word and believing in His promises that miracles begin to happen, and we certainly need a miracle to find hope in depression. This was the case for a Christian man that I met while speaking in Colchester. He had been backslidden for fifteen years, but decided that Sunday to come along to the meeting. For a long while he'd been struggling with depression and emptiness in his life. As I spoke about 'Overcoming The Storms of Life', God's promises came alive to him in a new way. He stepped forward at the invitation, coming to the front of the church, and repented of his sin, recommitting his life to the Lord.

In the same meeting was an unconverted, Russian student from Israel who was suffering the heartache of a broken marriage, and rejection by her own family. As she listened to God's word and started to believe in His promises, there came hope in the deep sadness of her life. She responded publicly that morning saying she wanted to become a Christian, and in doing so found new life and joy in Jesus Christ.

Fourthly –
Live with the Conviction that God is in Control
This really is a major key to those who feel imprisoned by depression and think their lives are falling apart. It will enable them, not only to be released, but to stay free as well.

Five times in these eight verses of Psalm 121 there is one consistent word that sums up a life lived with God in control. That word is, **'Lord'**. It is easy to sing 'He is Lord,' or to read it as ink on paper, but the Lordship of Jesus Christ is never truly tested until we are experiencing hard times. We need then to still declare it with confidence in these situations. One verse more than any other that expresses this so clearly, is Romans 8:28 –

> *'We know that in everything God works for good with those who love him, who are called according to his purpose.'*

There is always hope in depression when we live by this principle. It means that in the pain of life, we believe God

185

hasn't forgotten us, and He will bring something good out of our troubles.

A professor at a college in Richmond, Virginia was challenged by his students after he had addressed the morning assembly on the theme of Romans 8:28. They said, 'But professor, you don't really believe "all things work together for good," do you? All the pain and misery.' The professor replied, 'The things in themselves may not be good, but God can make them work together for good.' That afternoon he and his wife were out driving when they collided with another car. His wife was killed instantly and he himself was left a cripple. One day, several weeks later he sent for the college president and said, – 'Tell the students that Romans 8:28 still holds good.' When just a year later the professor died, his students had the verse inscribed on his tombstone. At the ceremony a local reporter asked why they had done this. They replied, 'It was inscribed in his convictions, why not on his tombstone?!'

There are many things that we don't understand about the sad experiences we pass through. One thing we can be sure of though is this, for every problem there is not only an answer, but also a purpose with God. We can trust Him to work out His divine plan knowing that He is the greatest Economist in the universe – He wastes nothing! The good work that He has begun, He is going to complete, even though at times what we are going through might make no sense at all. For example, if we were to visit a tapestry shop and look at those works of art on the reverse side, what we would see would be a hideous tangled mess of thread. It would appear a meaningless web of discolour and disharmony that had no form or sense. But if we were to view that same tapestry from the other side, then straight away we would see the beauty and skill of that woven picture.

For each of us when we just look at the 'down-side' of life, often we are not able to understand God's plan; it looks tangled and ugly. But some day we will see things as

186

He sees them. Then we will realise how God used even the dark threads to form the beauty and perfection of the completed pattern.